CREATIVE EXPERT FOR FORTNITERS

AN UNOFFICIAL GUIDE TO BATTLE ROYALE

CREATIVE EXPERT FOR FORTNITERS

MASTER COMBAT SERIES #5

JASON R. RICH

Sky Pony Press
New York

Sky Pony Press books may be purchased in bulk at special discounts for sales promotion, corporate gifts, fund-raising, or educational purposes. Special editions can also be created to specifications. For details, contact the Special Sales Department, Sky Pony Press, 307 West 36th Street, 11th Floor, New York, NY 10018 or info@skyhorsepublishing.com.

Sky Pony® is a registered trademark of Skyhorse Publishing, Inc.®, a Delaware corporation.

Visit our website at www.skyhorsepublishing.com.

10 9 8 7 6 5 4 3 2 1

Library of Congress Cataloging-in-Publication Data is available on file.

Cover design by Brian Peterson
Cover artwork by Getty Images
Interior photography by Jason R. Rich

Print ISBN: 978-1-5107-4975-7
E-Book ISBN: 978-1-5107-4980-1

Printed in the United States of America

TABLE OF CONTENTS

CREATIVE EXPERT FOR FORTNITERS

SECTION 1

FORTNITE: BATTLE ROYALE—THE BASICS

Fortnite: Battle Royale has become one of the most popular games in the world for a whole lot of really good reasons. It's fun, challenging, always evolving, offers many different gaming experiences, and it's free!

The game can be experienced on a Windows PC, Mac, PlayStation 4, Xbox One, Nintendo Switch, iPhone, iPad, or Android-based gaming system. If you switch between gaming systems, you'll discover that the Windows, Mac, PS4, Xbox One, and Nintendo Switch versions of the game are extremely similar.

Discover the Main Game Play Modes

When most gamers think of *Fortnite: Battle Royale*, they think of the "Battle Royale" game play modes.

While experiencing **Duos** mode, you and one other gamer (either an online friend or a stranger) can team up and compete against 98 other gamers during a match. You guessed

In Solo mode, for example, 100 gamers, each controlling one soldier, get airlifted by the Battle Bus to a mysterious island. The objective is to fight your way to become the last soldier alive at the end of the match and win #1 Victory Royale. To accomplish this, everyone else must perish.

it: the goal is to wind up being the last soldier standing when the match ends.

The Squads game play mode in Fortnite: Battle Royale *allows you to team up with three other gamers, and then fight as a squad against 24 other squads. The goal is to eliminate everyone else by the end of a match.*

On any given day, there is also a handful of other game play modes available. Each offers a totally different set of challenges, but all take place on the mysterious island that the game developers at Epic Games have created. Shown here, a Team Rumble match (a temporary game play mode) is about to begin.

Get Acquainted with the Mysterious Island

As you'll discover, there's a lot to see and experience on the mysterious island while trying to avoid the deadly storm.

This island is comprised of more than 20 unique points of interest that are labeled on the island map. This is what the island map looked like near the end of season 9. In between the various points of interest are countless other places to visit, explore, and fight in, although these places are not specifically listed on the island map.

Shown here is *The Block*, which is part of the Fortnite: Battle Royale *island map*. This is an area that Epic Games uses to feature content created by gamers who design incredible island maps (specifically to meet The Block's specifications) using Fortnite: Creative. As you'll discover, anyone can submit their maps to be featured within The Block, but out of the thousands of entries, only a few get accepted.

To help your soldier get around the island, there are a bunch of different types of vehicles at your disposal, along with a network of slipstreams (shown here) and ziplines. Like many other items, weapons, and locations in Fortnite, at the start of Season 10, slipstreams were vaulted in some game play modes, including Solo, but could make a return anytime in the future.

Exploration of the island during a match is essential, but equally important is engaging in combat, so you can eliminate the enemy soldiers you encounter. In order to prepare for each battle, you'll need to equip your soldier with the best selection of weapons, ammo, and loot items. As you can see, a soldier is using a Zipline here to quickly travel from one location to another. Several areas of the island feature a network of Zipline routes.

Depending on where you are on the island, you're also likely to encounter natural phenomenon, like Rifts or Geysers, that your soldier can leap into in order to travel around the island faster than on foot. A Geyser is shown here.

A Quadcrasher (shown here) is one of several types of vehicles that can often be found and then driven throughout the island. This type of vehicle is rugged, can go almost anywhere, and can hold multiple soldiers (if you're playing a Duos, Squads, or Team-oriented match, for example).

At any given time, there are more than one hundred different types of weapons available on the island, along with five different types of ammo, a selection of throwable explosive weapons, and other tools that can be used to help eliminate your adversaries.

As you travel around the island, you'll encounter small cities, suburban areas filled with single family homes, shopping malls, farms, factories, forests, underground mines, junkyards, camp grounds, areas with lakes, tall mountains, and wide open valleys, plus hundreds of stand-alone structures in between the popular points of interest (map locations).

Beware of the Deadly Storm

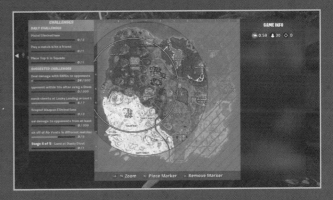

. . . And then there's the storm. Shortly after each match kicks off, a deadly storm forms somewhere on the island and then slowly expands and moves, making more of the island uninhabitable. As this happens, the surviving soldiers are forced into closer proximity. Eventually everyone remaining needs to fight in order to survive.

Check the island map periodically during each match to determine the size and location of the storm, so you can more easily avoid it.

As long as your soldier stays on the safe size of the storm, its harmful potential won't negatively impact your soldier. When you're playing Fortnite: Creative matches, some island maps disable the storm altogether, so this isn't something you'll need to contend with. However, it's certainly a factor when playing any of the Fortnite: Battle Royale game play modes (such as Solo, Duos, or Squads).

Building Is Often a Requirement for Success

In addition to using a wide range of buildings, structures, and objects found on the island to provide cover, by collecting resources (wood, stone, and metal), every soldier has the ability to build their own structures, protective barriers, ramps, and bridges. Building can be done almost anywhere on the island— indoors or outdoors.

Every Soldier Needs the Best Possible Arsenal of Weapons

The weapons at your soldier's disposal can also be used to destroy buildings and most solid objects found on the island. Based on where you are on the island, the environment, climate, and your surroundings will be very different.

Learn to overcome the challenges posed in each location, protect yourself from incoming enemy attacks, and determine when and how to go on the offensive (with the right weapons at your disposal). These are just a few of the skills you'll need to master if you want to achieve #1 Victory Royale.

Fortnite: Battle Royale Continues to Evolve

Once per week, Epic Games issues an update to Fortnite. Each update (referred to as a patch) might introduce new locations on the island map, new weapons, new loot items, new vehicles, and new challenges to overcome. At the same time, certain things within the game get "vaulted" (either temporarily or permanently removed from the game or certain game play modes), while other aspects of the game might get tweaked.

For example, when a weapon gets tweaked, it might be made even more powerful, or it could get nerfed, meaning that it's made weaker. These weekly changes are designed to keep you on your toes, and always provide new gaming experiences.

Then, once every two to three months, Epic Games launches a new gaming season. Each new season introduces some major changes to the game, and often includes significant alterations to the island map. When playing *Fortnite: Battle Royale*, while you can always expect new things to experience, those experiences and challenges are dictated by what Epic Games decides to offer.

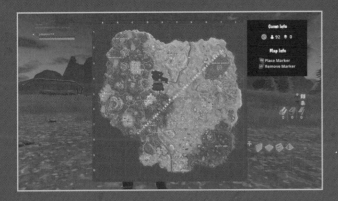

Shown here is what the island map looked like during season 3.

If you look closely, season 9 also brought about a bunch of alterations to the island map. Keep in mind, the evolution of the terrain never stops.

Here's how the island map appeared during season 5.

Create an Island from Scratch and Set the Rules of Engagement

Thanks to Creative mode, on any given day, there are thousands of unique island designs and gaming experiences available. These have been created and shared by your fellow *Fortnite* gamers. Some of these experiences are incredibly creative, unique, and extremely challenging. They are also available for free, if you know how to find them.

As you can see, the island changed a lot in conjunction with season 8, for example, and the changes continue to occur.

For those gamers with a great imagination, thanks to the game's Creative mode, the island itself can be re-designed and constructed from scratch by a gamer, and then the rules of engagement for a match can be customized and defined by that person. Custom-created games can be experienced by you and your friends anytime, but it's also possible to share your creations with the gaming public.

Shown here is the Fortnite: Creative *Hub. The soldier is standing in front of a Rift that'll transport him to a Featured Creator's island. This is one of the ways you can access island maps created by gamers whose work is being featured by Epic Games, or those who have become part of the Support a Creator program. (These gamers are able to generate Island Map Codes to share their maps with the public.) The island map shown here is called Covenant. Its Island Map Code is: 8472-1924-5936.*

The focus of this unofficial guide in the *Master Combat* series is to teach you the basics for creating your own awesome gaming experiences using the Creative mode built into *Fortnite*.

This unofficial guide shows you how to find and access original gaming experiences created by other gamers and showcases more than 25 truly awesome and unique island maps—some of which take place within familiar parts of the island, while others unfold in locations that gamers have created from scratch using the tools and resources available from Creative mode.

So whether you're looking to create your own *Fortnite* gaming experiences or want to experience new challenges developed by gamers (as opposed to the game developers at Epic Games), this unofficial strategy guide is packed with the information you'll need to get started.

Where to Find the Best Creative Gaming Experiences

Before you start tinkering with Creative mode to create your own island maps, take a look at what other gamers have done. As you'll soon discover, every day Epic Games showcases a different selection of maps created by gamers using Creative mode. For example, this Featured island map is called Baseball Mania! Its Island Map Code is: 8355-8358-0915.

However, there are many independent sources for finding and accessing the very best gamer-created *Fortnite: Creative* gaming experiences.

Some of these resources include:

- **Fortnite Creative HQ**—www. fortnitecreativehq.com
- **Fortnite Tracker Creative**—https:// fortnitetracker.com/creative
- **Games Rader**—www.gamesradar.com/ fortnite-creative-codes
- **Island Codes**—www.island-codes.com
- **PC Gamer**—www.pcgamer.coim/ fortnite-creative-codes

From these independent services, like Fortnite Creative HQ and others like them, you can learn about independent content creators and the original maps they've developed using Fortnite: Creative. Each one of these experiences has a unique title, description, video preview, and a unique 12-digit Island Map Code that you'll need to enter into the game in order to access that map.

During season 9, for example, Balloons had been vaulted from the Solo, Duos, and Squads game play modes of Fortnite: Battle Royale, but this transportation item remained available in the Creative game play mode.

Each time new tools are added, Creative content creators are able to use them to create even more incredible gaming experiences or improve upon Creative maps they've already created, published, and made available.

Often in conjunction with game updates and new gaming seasons, Epic Games adds new building tools and more creative assets into the Creative game play mode. Assets may include additional weapons, building/structures, vehicles, scenery, or other gaming elements from the current or past seasons of Fortnite: Battle Royale.

To discover when new features and functions have been added to the Creative game play mode, access the game's News section, or check out the official News section on the Fortnite website (www.fortnite.com/news). From within the game, to access the News screen, visit the Lobby, press the Menu button, and from the main game menu (shown here), scroll down and select the News option.

How to Use a Code to Find and Enter a Creative Map

Once you discover a code for a Creative game experience, follow these steps to access it:

1. Find a 12-digit numeric Island Map Code for the map you want to access and experience.
2. Launch *Fortnite: Battle Royale* on your favorite gaming system and click the Start button.
3. From the game's menu, select the Creative option.
4. If you want, drop into the Item Shop and purchase a new outfit or items.
5. Access the Locker and customize your soldier's appearance. Choose their outfit, back bling, Harvesting Tool design, glider design, which six emotes you'd like access to during the match, and which wraps you want to use to decorate your soldier's weapons and vehicles.
6. From the Lobby, invite online friends to join your Party if you plan to experience a multi-player island map.
7. Select the Play tab at the top of the screen to return to the Lobby. Make sure the Creative game play mode is selected (from above the Play button), and then click on the Play button.
8. From the Select a Server menu, choose one of the pre-created maps that have been created by your online friends (who are currently online), or scroll to the extreme right and highlight the Start a Server option. Click on the Launch button.
9. Your soldier will be transported to the Creative Hub.
10. Locate a Featured Island Rift and walk up to it. Do not enter into it, however.
11. When the title for the Featured Island appears, tap on the keyboard key or controller button associated with the Change Destination command. (On the PS4, use the square button.)
12. Replace the displayed Island Map Code with the code you want to use. Manually enter the 12-digit code using your keyboard or the onscreen virtual keyboard and your controller. You do not need to enter the dashes between the three sets of four digits as you're entering the code.

By entering an Island Map Code (also known as a Creative Code), you're able to transport your soldier to an island map that's been created from scratch by another gamer—not the folks at Epic Games. There are thousands of unique, challenging, and fun experiences to be had when you check out these custom maps.

13. Click on the Done button. With the newly entered code now displayed near the top-center of the screen, click on the Select Island button. Within a minute or two, your soldier will be transported to that island when they walk into the rift.

14. An information screen is displayed that describes the rules for the match. In addition to the match's title, you'll see how many players it's designed for, its difficulty level, the duration of each match, and other pertinent details. The match will begin momentarily. Click on the Start Game button to launch it immediately. But first, make sure you read the rules carefully. Some Creative matches and maps are designed for one gamer. Others can be experienced by up to 16 gamers at once.

15. If you've chosen a map that offers a multi-team challenge, before starting the game, you may need to press the Menu button and manually choose a team. This is only a requirement for some multi-team maps.

16. If you love the gaming experience that the creator developed, click on the Support a Creator option and then select that creator. Otherwise, prepare yourself to experience the match.

What you'll discover is that matches created by others using Creative mode offer a wide range of different experiences, many of which are unlike what the regular Solo, Duos, Squads, and Epic Games created game play modes have to offer. Obviously some of these matches will be better and more exciting than others.

When you enter some Creative matches, it'll immediately be obvious that its creator invested dozens or maybe hundreds of hours creating a truly unique gaming experience. Once you master that experience, however, simply find another that's equally if not more unique and challenging.

To exit out of a Creative match, press the Options key to access the Menu, and select either the Back to Hub or Leave Creative option. Back to Hub will transport you back to the Creative Hub, where you can choose a different match to participate in. The Leave Creative option will return you to the Lobby.

More Ways to Customize Your Gaming Experience

All highly skilled *Fortnite* gamers have a few things in common. They've spent countless hours playing *Fortnite: Battle Royale*'s various game play modes (Solo, Duos, Squads, etc.), and they've gotten to know the island's layout. They've also practiced working with the many different weapons, loot items, and vehicles available on the island, and often know where on the island they'll likely find what they need.

The very best *Fortnite* gamers have also fine-tuned their reflexes. They're able to interact with the game at lightning-fast speed. In addition to practice, they've memorized the game's controls and have perfected their muscle memory related to the version of *Fortnite: Battle Royale* (or *Fortnite: Creative*) they play. As a result, and without thinking, they know what keyboard key, mouse button or movement, or controller button to use at any given moment to achieve their objective.

After perfecting their gaming skills and developing their unique gaming style, the best *Fortniters* customize various options from the game's Settings menus, and in many cases, have upgraded their gaming equipment. This is done in hopes of maximizing their precision, control, and speed when controlling their soldier during matches.

Adjusting the Game's Settings

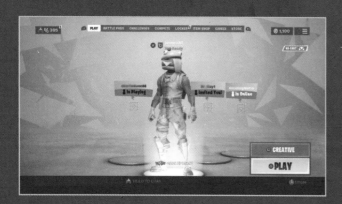

To access the Settings menu from the Lobby, click on the Game Menu icon that's displayed near the top-right corner of the screen on most gaming systems. This menu was given a new appearance toward the end of Season 9.

Notice the menu commands are now displayed on the right side of the screen, and the Social menu (for adding and inviting friends to matches) can be found on the left side of the screen. When the Game Menu is displayed, select the Settings option. It's now found near the top-right corner of the screen.

The Video Menu within Settings

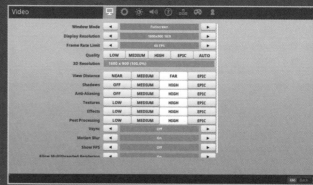

Displayed along the top of the Settings menu are a handful of command icons. Each represents a Settings submenu. The options available will vary, based on whether you're using a computer, console-based system, or mobile device. On a Windows PC (shown here), the menu icons (from left to right) include: Video, Game, Brightness, Audio, Accessibility, Input, Controller, and Account. From each of these submenus, there are a variety of options related to the game to tinker with.

PC and Mac gamers should select the **Video** tab on the Settings menu to adjust options related to the graphics. This is important especially if you have an older computer with a slower processor and graphics card. You want to optimize the game as much as possible to work with the computer you're using so *Fortnite* doesn't glitch while you're playing.

If you have a newer or higher-end PC, select the highest Display Resolution and Frame Rate Limit possible, and then for the Quality, View Distance, Shadows, Anti-Aliasing, Textures, Effects, and Post Processing options, choose the Epic options.

The Game Menu within Settings

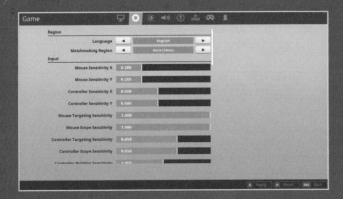

Whether you're using a PC, Mac, or console-based gaming system, the options available from the Game menu within Settings allow you to tweak the control you'll have over your soldier in the game while using a mouse/keyboard combo or a controller.

When connecting to the Epic Games gaming servers to play *Fortnite*, choose which region's servers to connect to. This directly impacts your connection speed when playing. From the top of the Game menu within Settings, choose your Matchmaking Region. Options include: Auto, North America—East Coast (NA-EAST), North America—West Coast (NA-WEST), Europe, Oceania, Brazil, or Asia. In parentheses next to each option is the current connection speed available, measured in milliseconds.

To have the smoothest, glitch-free gaming experience possible, choose the region that offers the fastest connection speed based on your current location. Your best bet is to choose the Auto option and allow the game to select the appropriate and fastest server. However, if you're based in one part of the planet and want to compete against gamers in another region, manually choose which region's servers you want to connect to, knowing that you will likely experience a slower connection to the distant server.

For the Sensitivity options listed below the Input heading, make small, incremental adjustments, play a few matches, and find the perfect settings for your personal gaming style and equipment. The goal is for your keyboard/mouse or controller to give you the fastest and most precise control possible.

As a newb, from below the Control Options heading of the Game menu, turn on features like Aim Assist, Edit Mode Aim Assist, Turbo Building, Controller Auto-Run, Auto Open Doors, and Auto Pick Up Weapons to help improve your speed when controlling your soldier during a match. Once you develop your muscle memory related to *Fortnite*, you can always go back and turn off some or all of these options.

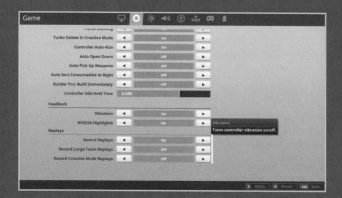

Some gamers turn on the controller-related Vibration feature (found below the Feedback heading of the Game menu) to add more realism to the game, so you literally feel the combat action in your hands as you're manipulating the controls. Some more advanced Fortniters turn off this feature, believing it slows down the game slightly and acts as a distraction. Whether or not you turn on this feature is a matter of personal preference.

The Audio Menu within Settings

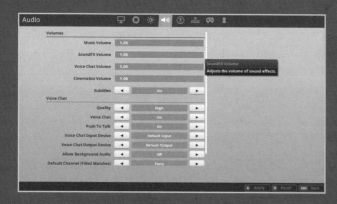

Regardless of which gaming system you're using to play, you'll quickly discover that sound plays an extremely important role in this game. For this reason, it's a good idea to boost the SoundFX Volume levels from the Audio menu (shown here on a PC), and lower or eliminate the Music Volume altogether to avoid its distraction.

Adjust the Input Menu When Using a Keyboard/Mouse Combo

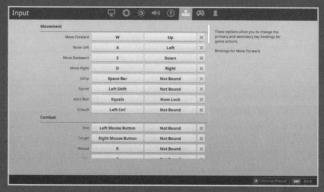

The Input menu allows you to customize the key bindings when using a keyboard and mouse to control the game. This means that you can adjust which keyboard key or mouse button you'll use to control each in-game feature, function, or action. As a newb, consider leaving the key bindings at their default settings.

However, as you develop your own gaming style, you may find it useful to change some of these settings to improve your reaction time and make the features, functions, or control settings you use frequently easier and faster to reach.

Customize Your Controller Options

When playing *Fortnite* with a controller (whether on a computer or console-based system), use the options offered from this Controller submenu within Settings to make subtle adjustments that could improve your reaction time, plus give you more precise aiming, for example.

When playing on a PC or Mac, first decide whether you'll be linking or connecting an Xbox One or Playstation 4 controller to your system. The next decision you'll need to make if you're a PC, Mac, Xbox One, PlayStation 4, or Nintendo Switch gamer is to choose the controller layout that best fits your personal gaming system. This decision should be based on your gaming system and personal preference.

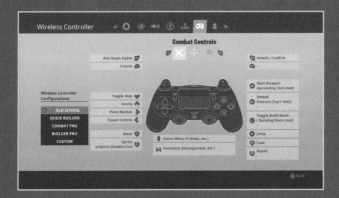

Whether you're playing on a console-based system (the PS4 is shown here) or on a computer, if you're using a gaming controller, you're able to choose between the Old School, Quick Builder, Combat Pro, Builder Pro, or Custom controller layout. (See the bottom-left corner of the screen.)

The Custom option allows you to manually adjust the key bindings for each button on the controller, while the other options allow you to choose between pre-created controller layouts. The goal is to match the controller-related settings you make to your personal gaming style and preferences.

Upgrade Your Gaming Hardware

The reaction time of your keyboard/mouse combo or controller directly impacts your success when playing *Fortnite*. For this reason, serious gamers often opt to upgrade their equipment to include a good quality gaming headset, along with a specialty gaming keyboard and mouse for their PC or Mac, and/or a more precision-oriented controller for their console-based gaming system.

These are optional purchases that you might want to make *after* you've played *Fortnite* for a while, you've tweaked the game controls (in Settings), and you believe your gaming abilities will improve with higher-end equipment.

For some gamers, a keyboard/mouse combo offers the most precise and responsive control options, especially if you're using a specialty gaming keyboard and mouse, such as those offered by Corsair (www.corsair.com), Logitech (www.logitechg.com), or Razer (www.razer.com/gaming-keyboards). The Razer Huntsman Elite keyboard for the PC ($199.99) is shown here.

Several companies, including Razer (www.razer.com/gaming-keyboards), offer one-handed, reduced-sized gaming keyboards, which feature fewer keys than a traditional keyboard, making it easier to reach only the keys needed to play a specific game, such as *Fortnite*.

The Razer Orbweaver Chroma, for example, is priced at $129.99 (US). In addition to awesome LED colored lighting effects, it offers thirty programmable keys (which includes twenty programmable mechanical keys). Priced at $34.95, the Fist Wizard One-Handed Gaming Keyboard (https://groovythingstobuy.com/products/fist-wizard-one-handed-gaming-keyboard-1) is a less expensive alternative.

Offering more precision than a standard console controller, several companies, such as SCUF Gaming (www.scufgaming.com), manufacture specialty Xbox One and PS4 controllers designed to cater to the needs of advanced gamers. The SCUF Impact controller for the PS4 ($139.95 US) is shown here. These controllers can also be used with a PC or Mac when playing Fortnite.

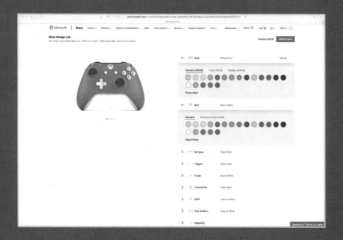

Microsoft offers a service that allows you to custom design a wireless or corded Xbox One controller. These controllers look different cosmetically but offer the same functionality as the controller that comes with the gaming system. The price varies, based on the options you choose. Check out https://xboxdesignlab.xbox.com/en-us to learn more about customizing an Xbox One controller's design.

Xbox One or PS4 console-based gamers can use the standard wireless controllers that came bundled with their gaming system, or upgrade to more advanced controllers. It's also possible to connect a gaming keyboard and mouse directly to a console-based system. The Turret for Xbox One gaming keyboard and mouse ($249.99 US) from Razer is shown here.

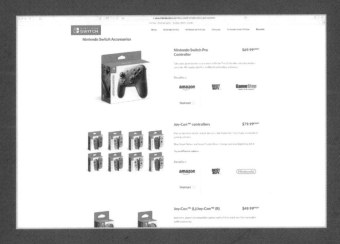

If you'll be experiencing Fortnite *on a Nintendo Switch gaming system, you'll have greater control over your soldier during matches if you upgrade to the Nintendo Switch Pro Controller ($69.99), as opposed to using the Joy-Con controllers that come bundled with the system. More creative gamers have figured out ways to connect a computer keyboard and mouse to a Nintendo Switch (while using the Dock and playing* Fortnite*). You'll find directions for how to do this on YouTube. (The Pro Controller does not work with the new Nintendo Switch Light gaming system. For more information about this system, visit: www.nintendo.com/switch/lite).*

Regardless of the gaming hardware you're using, memorize the controls for *Fortnite* and keep practicing using those controls so you develop your muscle memory for the game. When you're able to rely on your muscle memory, you'll be able to react faster without having to think about which key or button to press to accomplish specific tasks.

Don't Focus on the Game Settings Used by Top-Ranked Players

Many of the top-ranked *Fortnite: Battle Royale* gamers publish details about the game equipment they personally use, as well as the customizations they've made to the various Settings menu and submenu options. While this information is useful for reference, for

several reasons, you should not try to replicate another gamer's exact settings.

From the independent *Fortnite* Base website (https://fortbase.net/pro-players), for example, you can look up the player stats, ranking, gaming equipment list, and game-related settings for many of the best *Fortnite: Battle Royale* players in the world.

First, unless you have exactly the same gaming equipment and Internet connection speed used by the pro gamer, when you replicate their settings, you'll achieve different results on your own gaming system.

Second, every pro gamer tweaks the game based on their unique gaming style and experience level. If you play using a different style, or your reflexes and game-related muscle memory are not as developed as a pro gamer, copying their game settings will actually be detrimental to your success.

To discover the gaming equipment and customized settings used by top-ranked and pro *Fortnite: Battle Royale* gamers, check out these websites:

- **Best *Fortnite* Settings—**https://bestfortnitesettings.com/best-fortnite-pro-settings
- ***Fortnite* Base—**https://fortbase.net/pro-players
- ***Fortnite* Pro Settings & Config—**https://fortniteconfig.com
- **GamingScan—**www.gamingscan.com/fortnite-competitive-settings-gear
- **ProNettings.net—**https://prosettings.net/best-fortnite-settings-list

Experience *Fortnite: Creative* Using the Fastest Internet Connection Possible

To achieve the most reliable Internet connection speed on a computer or console-based gaming system, connect to the Internet using a physical Ethernet cable, as opposed to using a wireless (Wi-Fi) connection.

All current model Windows PCs and iMacs, as well as the Xbox One and PlayStation 4 have the ability to connect to the Internet via a wireless (Wi-Fi) connection or using a physical Ethernet cable that connects between your computer (or gaming console) and modem (or a router).

Many MacBook and MacBook Air laptop computers, for example, as well as the Nintendo Switch, do not have an Ethernet port built-in. In this case, an inexpensive Ethernet adapter can be purchased online or from a popular consumer electronics store. Keep in mind, a standard Ethernet cable (they come in many different lengths) also needs to be purchased separately.

Slow Internet often causes *Fortnite: Creative* to glitch during game play. When this happens, especially during an intense firefight or at the wrong moment, you could find your soldier getting eliminated from a match for no good reason.

Use a Gaming Headset

When engaged in combat, you'll want to clearly hear the sound effects the game generates, as well as the direction each sound is coming from. This includes the sound of footsteps, weapons fire, vehicles, doors opening and closing, building, and explosions, for example. The best way to ensure you hear *Fortnite*'s sound effects the way they were meant to be heard, and be able to communicate with your partner or squad mates during a match, is to invest in a good quality gaming headset.

Gaming headsets have built-in microphones. This type of optional accessory is available from a wide range of manufacturers. Some of the more popular gaming headsets used by top-ranked Fortnite: Battle Royale gamers come from companies like Logitech G (www.logitechg.com), HyperX (www.hyperxgaming.com/us/headsets), Razer (www.razer.com/gaming-headsets-and-audio), and Turtle Beach Corp. (www.turtlebeach.com).

Find Skilled Gamers to Play With

Having the best gaming gear will certainly give you an edge when playing *Fortnite*, but in addition to constantly working to improve your own gaming skills, you'll definitely want to team up with skilled and experienced partners or squad mates when experiencing various *Fortnite: Creative* maps.

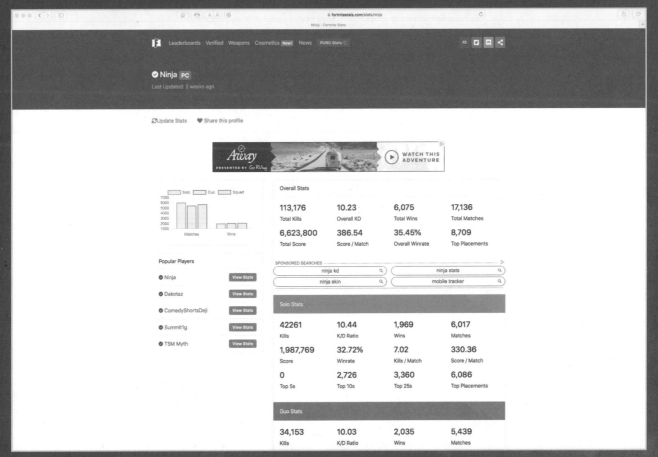

There are many independent websites, such as the Fortnite Stats & Leaderboard (https://fortnitestats.com), that allow you to quickly discover another gamer's Fortnite stats. In the Search field, simply enter the Epic Games username for any Fortnite: Battle Royale gamer to see their current stats as a player.

Playing with gamers who are better than you, or who have more experience, gives you a chance to learn new strategies as you follow someone else's lead during more intense combat situations.

Fortnite: Creative gives advanced and experienced gamers a forum to showcase island maps they've created from scratch in order to challenge themselves, their online friends, and in some cases, other Fortniters from around the world. To experience these custom-created maps, all you need to do is launch *Fortnite: Battle Royale*, select the Creative game play mode, and enter a special Island Map Code that'll unlock a specific map.

SECTION 2

LET'S GET CREATIVE

Approximately 90 years before Epic Games released *Fortnite: Battle Royale* and about 26 years before the Internet was even created, a song was written called "He's Got the Whole World in His Hands." However, when the *Fortnite: Creative* game play mode was introduced, the title of this song literally became a reality (at least in terms of a virtual world).

As you begin creating your own island (map) from scratch, think carefully about the rules of engagement you plan to allow during actual matches. What will the objective be? Based on this, you may want to adjust the layout of your map.

Will your island be hosting arena-style elimination matches, team-oriented matches, matches that have specific goals to achieve, or will it feature a maze-like design that soldiers need to navigate their way through while avoiding hazardous obstacles in their path? Once the island itself is designed, you'll be able to customize the rules of engagement for matches that'll take place on your island.

Working in Creative mode is really a three-step process. First, design and build your island map from scratch. Second, customize the rules of engagement for matches using the My Island menus. Third, invite online friends (or the gaming public if you're part of the Support A Creator program) to experience what you've created.

There Are Many Island Map Formats

There are many types of maps you can create, and map styles that other gamers have created that you can experience. You'll learn more about what sets these different style maps apart later in this guide.

Some of the most popular *Fortnite: Creative* map styles include:

- Adventures
- Death Matches (Solo or Team-Based Combat-Oriented Games)
- Deathruns/Obstacle/Parkour Courses
- Escape Challenges
- FFAs (Frantic Free-for-All Combat Experiences)
- Musical Maps
- Original Mini-Games
- Practice Arenas
- Prop Hunts (Hide and Seek Games with a Twist)
- Puzzle and Maze Maps
- Racing Simulations
- The Block Maps
- Zone Wars (Combat Challenges)

Start Designing and Building Your Own Island Map

From Fortnite's *main menu, or from the Select Game Play Mode menu that's accessed from the Lobby when playing* Fortnite: Battle Royale, *select the Creative game play mode, and the entire world of Fortnite is placed in your hands. Let your imagination run wild!*

To begin creating your own map from scratch, access the Creative Lobby (shown here) and select the Play option after visiting the Locker to customize the appearance of your soldier.

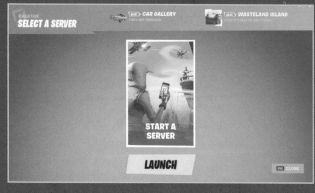

If none of your friends are currently online, the Select A Server screen will just show the Start A Server option. Use the Launch command to continue.

From the Select A Server menu, displayed are previews of worlds that have been created by your Epic Games Online Friends. These maps are from gamers who are online, so their maps are available for you to experience. Scroll to the right to see all of these pre-created maps and game play scenarios. When a slot is selected, either access the description of the map (to see which of your online friends is playing it) or select the Launch option to experience it yourself.

Within a minute or so, your soldier will be transported to the Creative Hub. From here, you're able to experience worlds created by other gamers that are being featured by Epic Games. To do this, walk up to and have your soldier enter any Featured Rift.

To begin creating your own map from scratch, scroll to the extreme right of the Select A Server menu screen (if necessary) and select the Start A Server option using the Launch command associated with it.

From the Hub, you're also able to enter into pre-created practice worlds which feature an island that's identical to what you'd find when playing Fortnite: Battle Royale.

Also within the Hub, every gamer has their own Rift. Have your character walk into your Rift. As you can see here, it's located between two staircases. If this is your first time in Creative mode, you'll be able to choose from an expansive menu of empty island styles. To access this menu, while facing the Rift (before entering it), select the Change Island option.

After selecting your island environment, within a few seconds you'll be transported to that empty island when you walk through the Rift. Shown here, the soldier is about to access the Black Grass Island 1 map. Your soldier will freefall onto the empty island map and land in its center. It's now time to start designing and building.

Scroll down within the Island Select menu and choose a default island style. As you're browsing through the Island Select menu, based on the default names of the islands, you can determine the type of terrain you'll discover there. Choose a terrain type that fits with your creative vision for the island map you plan to create from scratch. The default island you choose will determine its environment—not a location. For example, you can choose desert terrain, valleys, mountain areas, lake areas, or snowy terrain.

Building Requires Memory

If you've already started creating an island, its title will be listed here.

In the top-center of the screen is a Memory Units meter. At the start, it'll show you have one hundred thousand units of memory to work with. Based on which type of empty island you chose to land on, some of this memory may already be in use. Shown here, Meadow Island 1 was selected and even though nothing has been done to the island yet, 3,891 memory units are already being used.

Anytime you start working on a new island map, you'll discover some of your one hundred thousand units of memory is already gone. This is because the empty islands all have some basic landscaping items already in place, such as trees or rocks. To regain this memory, consider deleting the scenery items that are already in place.

Every Prefab structure, Gallery item, or Device you place on your island will utilize some memory. For example, if you were to add a Tilted Tower Clock Tower to your map from the Prefab menu, the first clock tower you add would utilize 1,797 memory units (out of your allocated one hundred thousand units).

Any additional and identical clock towers you add to your map would require just 252 memory units. Even adding a chest or Loot Llama to your island will require memory (about twenty memory units each).

As you're building, keep an eye on the memory usage meter and make sure you'll have enough memory to create the map you envision before you invest many hours only to discover you can't finish your map because you've run out of available memory.

Take Your Time and Be Patient

One of the most important things you need to understand about *Fortnite: Creative* is that it takes time to build a really awesome and functional map, so be patient. Especially if you start working with individual building tiles from the Gallery menus, designing and building individual structures from scratch can be very time consuming.

It's common to read in the descriptions for island maps created by other people that they spent forty hours or more a building a single map. Sure, you can probably build a basic map using Prefabs in fifteen to thirty minutes, tinker with the My Island menu options, and then start playing matches on your island within an hour. However, what you create will not be as intricate (either visually or from a game play standpoint) as something that a gamer who invested fifty hours or more to design will wind up with.

While Building, You'll Need to Switch Between Create and Play

While in Creative mode, there are two main activities—Create and Play. In the lower-right corner of the screen are your soldier's Harvesting Tool and Smartphone icons. When the Harvesting Tool is selected, this indicates you're in Play mode. You can explore your island freely. Select the Smartphone icon to switch to Create (Building) mode (shown here).

When in Create mode and designing your island map from scratch, the building you do using the tools provided is separate from the building soldiers can do using wood, stone (brick), and metal tiles when actually participating in matches.

In Play mode, you're free to explore your island as you're designing it. Your soldier can walk, run, or fly around, for example. This mode is different from actually experiencing (playing) the match as a gamer, however. To do this, once the map is completed and you've customized the menu options associated with the My Island submenus, return to the Game submenu of My Island, and choose the Start Game option.

and a structure from what was once Lazy Links.

Your building tools are divided into a handful of categories. They're labeled Prefabs, Galleries, Devices, Weapons, Consumables, and Chest. Many of these categories have an ever-growing selection of sub-categories. Each contains content you'll use to create your island map.

Building with Prefabs

The benefit to working with Prefabs is that it's easy to select and place pre-created buildings and structures onto your island. These have all been designed by the folks at Epic Games, and at some point in *Fortnite: Battle Royale*'s history, each has been featured somewhere on the island.

Each Prefab building or structure you add to your island map requires memory units. Additional memory units will be required if you plan to edit the Prefab building or add onto it using items from the Gallery menus.

Keep in mind, Prefabs offers buildings and structures from many different gaming seasons, so some of your pre-created building/structure options may have been vaulted from *Fortnite: Battle Royale*. As a result, on your own island map you could theoretically place a building from the original Tilted Towers between a building from Neo Tilted

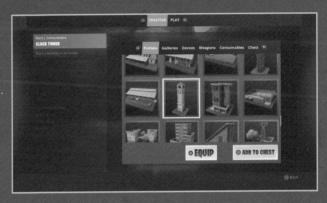

After selecting the Prefabs tab near the top of the screen, you'll see individual buildings. Each is a pre-created building or structure that'll probably look familiar, since it's a building that's been featured at some point on the island when playing *Fortnite: Battle Royale*. When in Creative mode, you're able to choose any single, pre-created building or structure and place it anywhere, plus add as many of that building or structure as you'd like onto your island map, assuming there's enough memory units remaining to do so.

Using your controller or mouse, highlight one building or structure from this menu screen, such as the Village Town Hall, and select the Equip option. Next, exit out of this menu by pressing the Back button on your controller or keyboard.

You'll find yourself back on your empty island map. Taking up one of your soldier's Inventory slots, to the right of their Harvesting Tool and Smartphone, you'll see the building or structure you just selected. Highlight and select this Inventory slot. In your soldier's hand, you'll now discover an orb that contains the building or structure you've selected.

With the building or structure orb in your soldier's hand, press the Build button, and within a second or two, that building will be placed on your island in the location you selected. Your soldier will be placed in the center of the newly built structure. Using the directional controls, you're able to have your soldier walk or run around the island, so you can see what you're building, as you build it, from your soldier's perspective.

Using the aiming tool that's displayed near the center of the screen, decide the exact location where you want to place the selected Prefab building or structure.

Another option for getting around the island when in Creative mode (while building your island) is to fly. On the left side of the screen the HUD (heads-up display) shows what mouse/keyboard or controller button to press in order to fly. On a PS4, for example, as you can see, you'd double-tap the "X" button.

If you need a bigger and more detailed view of your custom island, beyond what's seen on the mini-map, press the Island Map button on your mouse/keyboard or controller.

As soon as your soldier begins flying, the HUD display offers a handful of additional commands that are displayed on the left side of the screen. These include: Exit Fly, Fly Up, Fly Down, Inventory, Phase (Hold) [Off], and Flight Speed [2.0x]. Use these commands to move around and interact with your island and its contents as you're creating it.

With one building now built, you're ready to place additional buildings, structures, and other items, one at a time, onto your island map. Keep in mind, additional items can be placed inside any pre-created structure, or using the Gallery building items available, you can now customize the Prefab structure by adding or removing pieces of it.

As you can see here, the Cut and Paste commands were used twice, and two additional windows were placed on the second floor of the Village Town Hall.

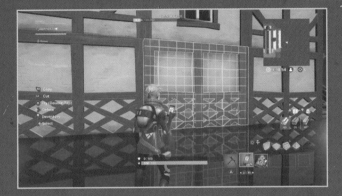

Once a Prefab building/structure has been placed on your island map, it's possible to select one tile or object from that structure and delete, move, or duplicate it. This allows you to customize that building in a way that often uses less memory units than adding items/tiles from the Gallery.

Return to the Creative menu. One at a time, choose other individual buildings to place on your island map while the Prefab tab is selected. There are well over 100 pre-created buildings and structures to choose from. Epic Games regularly adds new buildings and structures to the Prefabs menu. Shown here, the Village Clock has been selected.

Shown here, a window tile of the Village Town Hall has been selected. The HUD on the left side of the screen shows six options, including: Copy, Cut, Fly (Double Tap), Delete, Inventory, and Select. These options allow you to work with that one tile. For example, you can copy and then paste that tile in another location to add more windows to the structure.

The selected Village Clock has been placed next to the Village Town Hall on the island map.

You're given a lot of freedom when building and designing your island using Prefabs. For example, you can place buildings or structures directly next to each other, on top of each other, or even inside one another. The possibilities are truly limitless. Shown here, the Pueblo Bell Tower has been placed on the roof of a Neo Tilted Gas Station.

Working with Galleries

Prefabs are pre-created buildings and structures. Galleries contain an assortment of themed building tiles and items that you can mix-and-match, one at a time, to create or modify any type of building or structure you choose. Your options are only limited by the one hundred thousand memory units available and your imagination.

Because you're literally working with one tile at a time, building a detailed structure can become a rather time consuming and tedious process, so be patient! The results, however, can be pretty incredible from a visual standpoint. Some of the best Creative maps featured later in this guide were designed from scratch using mainly tiles and items from the Galleries menus. If you're in a hurry, however, work with just Prefab options.

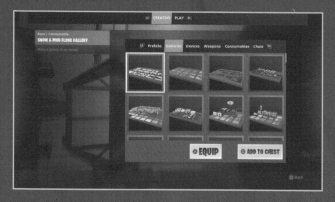

As you scroll through the Gallery menu, you'll discover a wide range of themed floor options.

Many of the other galleries contain a section of themed wall, ceiling, window, and door tiles. Each theme comes from a specific map location or Point of Interest from Fortnite: Battle Royale. Shown here is the Neo Tilted Durrr Burger Gallery.

Keep scrolling downwards when viewing the Galleries menu to discover selections of themed scenery tiles, like this Holiday Gallery. As with the items in any Gallery, you can choose one item at a time, rotate, and/or resize it, and then place it where you want on the map. Shown here, all items in the Holiday Gallery have been placed on the island map.

Don't forget landscaping! The island you're creating from scratch can contain any assortment of trees, bushes, rock formations, lighting, fireworks, train tracks, and even colored cubes (that you construct into whatever design you desire). Mixing and matching décor from different parts of the Fortnite: Battle Royale island is what Creative mode is all about. Shown here is the Nature Tree Gallery.

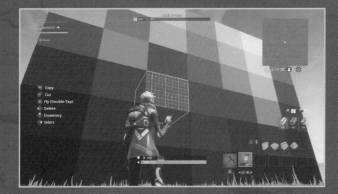 

After choosing a blue-colored cube from the Gallery called Cube Gallery Large, the item was selected and copied.

While the blue cube is selected, using the commands available on the HUD display (left side of the screen), it's possible to do things like Paste, Push, Pull, Grow, and Shrink the cube before placing it on the island map. This can be done with any item from the Gallery or any tiles (or building/structure) from the Prefab menu.

Shown here, the same blue cube has been resized, repositioned, and then placed multiple times on the island map. This ability to resize and rotate items/tiles is what allows gamers to create elaborate, original-looking statues and structures within their maps.

Of course, you can start by placing a Prefab building on your island, and then customize it using different types of building and decorating tiles from Galleries. As you choose individual items or tiles from the Gallery menus, each can be rotated, replicated, and placed anywhere on your island map. However, what really gives you design flexibility is the ability to re-size (scale) and then rotate each item or tile.

After choosing a specific Gallery that contains items you want to add to your island map, find an open area on your island that won't overlap with the area where you're currently building, and temporarily place the entire contents of a Gallery on your island. Pick and choose which items/tiles you want to use while building. Then, when you're done with that Gallery, delete the items you don't need. Doing this can speed up your building process and give you a pallet of related items/tiles to work with.

Working with Devices

Making your island look awesome using Prefab buildings and structures, as well as

items and tiles from the Gallery, is only the beginning. Part of what makes a custom island map exciting to experience later during matches is its interactivity.

Check out the Devices menu to discover many interactive "devices" that you can place anywhere within your island—either inside or outside of buildings or structures you've already placed. Devices are listed one at a time, each in their own slot. Using the Equip command, choose one a time, and then return to your island to place that item in one or more locations.

Some of the Devices available allow you to make your island interactive in ways that are not possible when playing Fortnite: Battle Royale. *For example, you can use Triggers to kick off events or activate other devices you place on the island. Shown here, two Launch Pads have been placed on the ground of the island map.*

The Devices you place on your island can also be useful for making certain types of rules of engagement possible once you create custom matches that'll take place on your island map. For example, you can place Capture Areas, and various types of "Spawners" (used to make specific or random types of weapons, computer-controlled enemies, or items appear during matches).

Depending on the type of Spawner you add to your island, and then how you customize (program) each of them, a Spawner will cause specific weapons, healing items, or loot items to appear at a designated spot and at a specific time interval during each match.

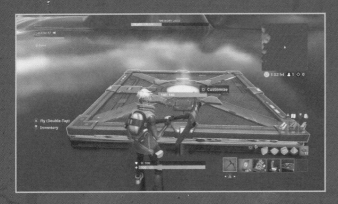

An Item Spawner allows specific or random items to appear on the island, at the location you place the Spawner tile, at an interval you determine.

Use a Player Spawner to determine where soldiers will materialize on your island map at the start of a match, or the location they'll respawn during a match after they've been eliminated. (Assuming respawning is something you permit when setting up the rules of engagement for matches.)

Many of the functional vehicles you already know from playing *Fortnite: Battle Royale*, such as ATKs, Quadcrashers, X-4 Stormwing

airplanes, Driftboards (hoverboards), and Ballers can be placed on your island at specific locations, or be set up to spawn during a match in the locations and at the time intervals you specify. Depending on the type of match you're creating, a vehicle will come in handy if a gamer needs to cover a lot of terrain or travel through a maze or obstacle course. Functioning vehicles will be less useful if your matches will take place in a confined space.

A functioning vehicle is one that soldiers can drive or ride in, while a decorative vehicle can be used for shielding (if a soldier stands or crouches behind it), but it can't be driven. Decorative vehicles (shown here is Car Gallery A from the Galleries menu in Fortnite: Creative) can also be smashed using the Harvesting Tool to collect Resources (metal), if you opt to allow building on your island during matches.

Shown here is the Gallery called Car Gallery B. It offers a different selection of decorative (undrivable) vehicles than Car Gallery A.

Four different Vehicle Spawner tiles (which generate drivable vehicles) have been placed here, next to each other. When adjusting the My Island menu options, you can determine whether or not the Spawner tiles themselves, or just the vehicles, will be displayed on your island during a match.

Various types of Traps can be placed anywhere on your island map and used the same way as when playing Fortnite: Battle Royale, *except you can add them to your island prior to a match. Traps can also be made during a match using an Item Spawner or added to the inventory of a chest or Loot Llama that a soldier can open during a match. Four different types of Trap tiles are shown here, including a Chiller, Damage Trap, Poison Dart Trap, and Speed Boost Trap.*

Some items, like Firepits, can be placed on your island map whenever you desire. These too are used to replenish a soldier's Health in exactly the same way as they are when playing *Fortnite: Battle Royale.*

Each item you place requires some of the available one hundred thousand memory units, so if you're running low on memory units when creating your island map, only add

items that'll help you achieve the playability goals you have for your island map.

Each Device offered within Creative mode has some type of interactive purpose. Some can impact game play or can be used during combat, while others are used to set up specific objectives or tasks within the island map you create.

Sentries (silver-colored soldiers that are computer-controlled) can be placed in or around buildings or structures (or anywhere else for that matter) to serve as an automated guard capable of automatically attacking soldiers that approach. By checking out various maps that other gamers have created, you'll discover that Devices like Sentries and Traps have been used in very interesting and creative ways.

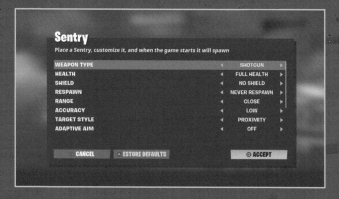

After placing a Sentry tile, have your soldier walk up to it and use the Customize command to access this Sentry customization menu. As you can see, it allows you to determine how the Sentry will function during a match. For example, select what weapon the Sentry will have, along with their Health and Shield level, Respawn rate, firing Range, and shooting Accuracy.

An Example of Sentries and Traps Being Used in *Fortnite: Creative*

The Creative map described here uses several types of Devices to make it function, including a Player Spawner, several Item Spawners, Sentries, illuminated Pyramids from the Collectible Gallery (found within the Devices menu), and Damage Traps.

These are just a few of the interactive Devices you can add to your own island maps. Deciding which Devices to use is one important decision, but then you need to determine how they'll be used, since many of them can be customized.

There are many ways to incorporate Sentries and Traps, for example, in your island maps. The Master Combat Series Demo Deathrun map (Map Code: 7165-8631-4334) is an example of a one-player deathrun that's rather short, but nevertheless a big challenge.

The goal is to collect ten illuminated Pyramids while trying to get from one end of the corridor to the other in less than three minutes.

In your path are several overhead Traps. Multiple Sentries have also been placed along the path a soldier must follow—each is programmed separately to react to a gamer's soldier a bit differently. During this match, you're only able to respawn three times before the match ends. You can't destroy the structures and no building is permitted. As you make your way through this Deathrun, pay attention to how Sentries are used. Because each was programmed differently, some are easier to eliminate than others. Some make multiple appearances (respawn) after being defeated, while others do not.

Grab a weapon right away and be ready to shoot. Just after your soldier begins the match, there's an Item Spawner that spits out Health- and Shield-related items. These can be useful. Next, proceed through the doorway and grab a weapon, so you're ready to fight the Sentries (shown here).

Some of the Sentries have more powerful weapons at their disposal and respawn frequently, while others won't reappear after they've been defeated. The map was designed so the Sentries would cause enough of a distraction and challenge to keep the gamer from collecting all ten of the Pyramids that are necessary to win.

This sample map also shows that you don't need to create a map that's extremely large or complex in order to make the game play challenging and fun.

Add Weapons to Your Island

Just about every weapon ever released in *Fortnite: Battle Royale*—including most weapons that have been vaulted—are available in Creative mode. As you're designing and constructing your own island map, weapons can be placed in several ways.

From the Weapons menu, notice that the Legendary weapons are displayed first. Scroll down to see the Epic, Rare, Uncommon, and Common ranked weapons that are available.

The very first "weapon" displayed within the Weapons menu (in the top-left corner) is not actually a weapon. It's the Prop-O-Matic gun. This is used in Prop Hunt matches. When this weapon is pointed at almost any item or object on the map, the soldier's appearance who is holding the Prop-O-Matic will transform into that item. This can be used as a disguise.

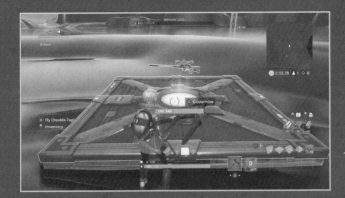

Set up Weapon (Item) Spawners to make specific or random weapons appear at specific locations during a match, at the time interval(s) you choose. To do this, select the Item Spawner tile from the Devices menu, and place Item Spawner tile(s) on your map. Next, drop items from your soldier's inventory onto the Spawner tile while you're creating the island map. Only the items you place on the Item Spawner tile while creating the map will appear on your island during actual matches that you and your friends are playing.

Place any assortment of weapons (and ammo) within chests, and then place one or more chests wherever you wish on the island. Placing items within a chest (or Loot Llama), and then adding chests (or Loot Llamas) to the island requires fewer memory units than placing multiple weapons individually. If you choose to create chests or Loot Llamas while using Creative mode, then while accessing the Weapons menu, select and highlight one weapon slot at a time. Instead of pressing the Equip button, press the Add To Chest button. Notice that in the top-right corner of the screen, a number (indicating how many weapons you've selected) is now displayed in conjunction with the Chest tab.

Once you've selected and used the Add To Chest command on all of the weapons and items you want to place into a chest or Loot Llama, switch to the Chest menu by selecting the Chest tab. The current inventory of what you selected to add to the chest is displayed. At this point, use with the Create Llama or Create Chest command to place the inventory of weapons into a Loot Llama or Chest.

Use the cell phone to position the chest or Loot Llama you just created. Choose the exact location where you want to place the each chest. When you're done, switch to the soldier's Pickaxe (shown here). In this case, the chest has now been added to the map and can be searched when experiencing the map as a player.

At this point, you can place as many of the same Loot Llamas or chests as you'd like on your island. Each will contain the same inventory of weapons. If you want to create chests or Loot Llamas that contain a different inventory selection, repeat the steps just outlined, but be sure to clear the Chest inventory first using the Remove command found on the Chest Inventory screen.

How to Program a Weapon/Item Spawner

An Item Spawner is a tile that you can place anywhere on your island. Once you custom program that Item Spawner while in Creative mode, you're able to determine what weapons (or items) it'll spawn and how often it'll function during a match.

Once the Item Spawner tiles are placed and you've provided inventory to them, one at a time, have your soldier face them and select the Customize command.

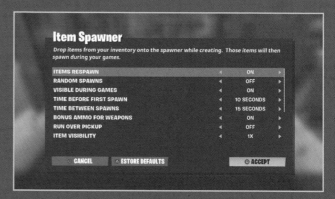

The Item Spawner Customizer menu looks like this. Starting with the Items Respawn menu, adjust each item.

Place as many Item Spawners as you'd like, wherever you want on your island. Using weapons or items from the Weapons or Consumables menus, select which items you want the Spawner to generate during a match and drop them onto the Spawner tile.

Programming Options for an Item (Weapon) Spawner

Here's a summary of what each Item Spawner menu option is used for. Once you make changes to the Item Spawner menu, be sure to use the Accept command to save your changes. Keep in mind, each Item Spawner you place on your island needs to be customized separately.

MENU COMMAND	DESCRIPTION	AVAILABLE SETTINGS
Items Respawn	Once the Item Spawner is used once, determine whether or not it can be used again during the same match.	On—Allows the Item Spawner to be used multiple times during a match. Off—Allows the Item Spawner to be used just once per match.
Random Spawns	Determines the order of items (including weapons) that will spawn during a match.	Off—The order items spawn is not randomized. Random—The order items spawn is random. No Repeats—The order items spawn is random, but with no repeats until all of the items/weapons in that Item Spawner's inventory have been spawned once.
Visible During Games	Determine whether or not the Item Spawner tile itself will be visible during a match, or if only the items it spawns will appear on the island at the designated time(s).	On—The Item Spawner remains visible on the island during a match at all times. Off—The Item Spawner remains invisible at all times. Only the items and weapons spawned by the Item Spawner become visible.
Time Before First Spawn	Starting at the beginning of each match, this setting determines the first time the Item Spawner will make an item (or weapon) appear.	Instant, 1 Second, 2 Seconds, 3 Seconds, 4 Seconds, 5 Seconds, 10 Seconds, 15 Seconds, 20 Seconds, 25 Seconds, 30 Seconds, 45 Seconds, 1 Minute, 1.5 Minutes, 2 Minutes, 3 Minutes, 4 Minutes, or 5 Minutes
Time Between Spawns	This setting determines the time lapse between item (or weapons) spawns by that Item Spawner.	1 Second, 2 Seconds, 3 Seconds, 4 Seconds, 5 Seconds, 10 Seconds, 15 Seconds, 20 Seconds, 25 Seconds, 30 Seconds, 45 Seconds, 1 Minute, 1.5 Minutes, 2 Minutes, 3 Minutes, 4 Minutes, or 5 Minutes

MENU COMMAND	DESCRIPTION	AVAILABLE SETTINGS
Bonus Ammo for Weapons	This option allows you to determine if each weapon that's spawned will include just one clip full of ammo, or if bonus ammo will be provided with the weapon.	On—Bonus ammo is provided with each weapon. Off—Just one clip's worth of ammo is provided with the weapon.
Run Over Pickup	Items or weapons that are created by the Item Spawner can be picked up automatically when a soldier walks over or drives over the Item Spawner.	On—Available item(s) or weapon(s) automatically get picked up by the soldier. Off—The soldier must manually pick up the available item(s) or weapon(s).
Item Visibility	Use this setting to determine how the items/weapons are displayed. If you choose 1x, for example, only one item at a time will be displayed. If an item/weapon does not get picked up, but another one spawns, the first item will disappear and be replaced by the newly spawned item/weapon.	1x, 2x, 3x, 4x, or 5x
Enabled on Game Start	This option allows you to determine whether or not the Item Spawner will activate automatically at the start of a match, or if something else needs to happen first. For example, you can set it up so a Transmitter or Receiver needs to be used by a soldier in order to activate the Item Spawner during a match.	Enabled—The Item Spawner will begin functioning immediately at the start of a match. Disabled—The Item Spawner will not function at the start of a match and will wait until a specific event or action (that you pre-select) occurs during a match.
Enable/Disable Receiving From	Used for creating "if/then" or "true/false" scenarios to be experienced during matches.	No Channel— Choose between Channel 1 and Channel 8
Spawn Item When Receiving From	Used for creating "if/then" or "true/false" scenarios to be experienced during matches.	No Channel— Choose between Channel 1 and Channel 8
Cycle to Next Item When Receiving	Used for creating "if/then" or "true/false" scenarios to be experienced during matches.	No Channel— Choose between Channel 1 and Channel 8

Keep Soldiers Healthy by Providing Consumables

In addition to deciding what weapons/ammo will be made available on your island during a match, you're also be able to choose the exact assortment and inventory of consumable items that will be offered during a match.

As you can see from the Consumables menu, just about every non-weapon item ever introduced into Fortnite: Battle Royale *is available to you, including items that were long ago vaulted.*

Items offered from the Consumables menu can be placed on the island manually using Item Spawner tiles, at specific locations you choose, or they can be added to chests or Loot Llamas (which can then be placed anywhere on your island but will need to be opened by a soldier during a match).

Consumable items fall into one of several categories, including:

- **Ammunition**—There are five types of ammo used by the various weapons in the game. These include Light Bullets (used by Pistols and other low-caliber weapons), Medium Bullets (used by Assault Rifles and other weapons with a mid-range reach), Large Bullets (used by Sniper Rifles and similar long-range weapons), Shells (used by Shotguns), and Rockets (used by projectile explosive weapons, such as Rocket Launchers, Guided Missile Launches, or Grenade Launchers).

- **Health Replenishment Items**—Used to replenish a soldier's Health meter. These include: Bandages, Med Kits, Slurp Juices, and Chug Jugs.

- **Resources**—Wood, stone (brick), and metal bundles used for building during a match.

- **Shield Replenishment Items**—Used to activate or replenish a soldier's Shield meter during a match. A soldier's Shield meter typically starts off at zero. Once activated, it can go up to 100. Then each time a soldier is injured as a result of weapons fire or an explosion, some of their Shield meter gets depleted. Once their Shields are gone, a soldier's Health meter gets depleted by the damage. Shield Replenishment items include: Small Shield Potions, Shield Potions, Slurp Juices, Chug Jugs, and Chug Splashes.

- **Throwable Explosive Weapons**— These are items that get carried in a soldier's inventory and can be tossed at a target, often to create an explosion. Explosive weapons can also destroy solid objects (including buildings, structures, and vehicles), plus cause damage to soldiers. Throwable Explosive Weapons include: Grenades, Clingers, Smoke Grenades, Shadow Bombs, Stick Bombs, Boogie Bombs, Impulse Grenades, Shockwave Grenades, Bottle Rockets, Dynamite, and Remote Explosives.

- **Tool-Related Items**—There is a growing selection of items that can be used in combat to help a soldier survive longer during a match, or as a transportation alternative to get around the island. These include: Port-A-Forts, Port-A-Fortresses, Presents, Sneaky Snowmen, Bushes, Rift-To-Go items, Balloons, Glider items, Grappler items, and Jetpacks.

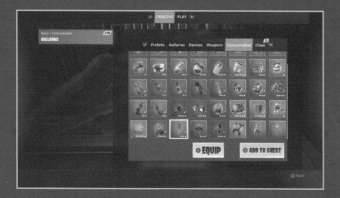

When you highlight and select a Consumable item from the Consumables menu (on the right side of the screen), a description of what that item is used for during a match is displayed on the left side of the screen.

You Decide Where Chests and Loot Llamas Are Placed and What They Offer

As you're choosing items from the Weapons or Consumables menu, using Item Spawner tiles gives you the option to manually place each thing on the island, so it appears during a match on the ground, out in the open.

One of your other options as an island map creator is to choose exactly what items and weapons get placed within chests and/or Loot Llamas, and then decide where and how many chests and Loot Llamas get placed on the island and made available during matches.

Each chest or Loot Llama you place on your island can contain the same collection of items or weapons, or you can manually choose the inventory of each chest and Loot Llama separately while in Creative mode.

Customize Your Island's Rules of Engagement

Using the tools offered in Creative mode and the items offered by the Prefabs, Galleries, Devices, Weapons, Consumables, and Chests submenus, you're able to design and build a fully customized island map. The design choices you make, however, should be based on how you plan to utilize the island once it's been built.

Once your own island map has been designed and built, access the Menu and select the My Island option to adjust the rules of engagement for matches that'll take place on it.

Along the top of the My Island menu are six tabs. They're labeled: Game, Game Settings, UI Settings, Island Tools, Description, and Permissions. You'll want to visit each of the submenus and adjust the options offered within them to create a match experience that's unique, challenging, and that adheres to the rules you envision.

Keep in mind, the folks at Epic Games are constantly expanding the toolset available in Creative Mode. By the time you start using this game play mode, you may discover additional tools, features, and functions have been added, while others may have been vaulted.

The Game Menu

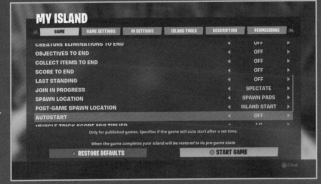

Here's a summary of what each of the options available from the Game submenu are used for when it comes to customizing the rules of engagement for the matches that'll take place on your island.

After making changes to any of the My Island submenus, if you want to revert all of the menu options to their default settings, use the Restore Defaults command that's displayed in the bottom-left corner of the screen.

To save the changes made to each submenu setting, be sure to use the Apply command (found near the bottom-right corner of the screen) before leaving the submenu.

MENU OPTION	DESCRIPTION	SETTING OPTIONS
Voice Chat	Determine if gamers visiting your island will be able to chat with each other during matches.	**All**—Gamers will be able to chat with everyone experiencing the match, including allies and enemies. **Team**—Gamers will only be able to chat with their team members. **None**—The chat feature will be disabled during matches, so no communication can take place.
Teams	Use this option to determine whether or not gamers will each work alone when engaged in a match or be part of a team.	**Free for All**—Each gamer works alone. There are no teams. **Cooperative**—All players participating in the match are part of the same team and work together to achieve specific objectives. **Number of Teams**—Based on the number of players allowed in each match, this option allows you to determine how many teams the gamers will be divided into. Options range from two to 16 teams, but there's also a Custom option.

MENU OPTION	DESCRIPTION	SETTING OPTIONS
Spawns	When playing a Solo match in *Fortnite: Battle Royale*, once a gamer is eliminated from the match, they're done and unable to respawn. In other game play modes, players can respawn multiple times during a match. This feature allows you to determine how many times a gamer can respawn during matches that take place on your island.	**Infinite**—An unlimited number of respawns is possible. **1 through 10**—Choose exactly how many times each gamer can respawn during a single match after being eliminated.
After Last Spawn Go To	Using this option, determine what happens to gamers after they're permanently eliminated from a match (and no longer able to respawn).	**Spectator**—They go into Spectator mode and can watch the rest of the match. **Team Number** (1 through 16)—The player is removed from their existing team and becomes part of another team that you specify.
Total Rounds	Determine how many Rounds each match will include. At the start of each Round, the environment you created on the island resets.	Enter the number of Rounds you want in your matches, between one and 100.
Team Rotation	Adjust how many Rounds will take place before teams are rotated. In an arena-style game, where each team has their own side of the island, this home turf will switch as a result of each rotation.	**Disabled**—There's no rotation between Rounds. **Every Round**—Teams are rotated after each Round. **Every Other**—Teams are rotated every other Round.
Time Limit	Select how long each match will last.	**None**—Gamers must achieve a specific objective that you pre-determine for a match to end. **Between 1 and 20 Minutes**—You set the specific time length of each match.
Fastest Time Win	After all of the Rounds are completed, the team or player who completed the match's objectives in the lowest time (the fastest) is declared the winner.	**Disabled**—This feature does not apply to your matches. **Enabled**—This feature applies to your matches.

MENU OPTION	DESCRIPTION	SETTING OPTIONS
Eliminations to End	Determine how many eliminations a gamer or a team must achieve for the match to end.	**Off**—The number of eliminations does not cause the match to end. **Between 1 and 1,000**—Achieving a specific number of eliminations that you pre-set determines when a match will end.
Creature Eliminations to End	Using the Creature Spawner that's offered in the Devices menu, you can add computer-controlled enemy creatures (such as zombies, monsters, or sentries) to your island that gamers must defeat. This option determines how many creatures need to be defeated to end the match.	**Off**—Defeating creatures has no impact on the match or its overall objectives. **Between 1 and 1,000**—Determine specifically how many computer-controlled creatures need to be eliminated to win a match.
Objectives to End	After setting specific objectives to complete during a match, you can determine how many of those objectives must be completed in order to win.	**Off**—No objectives need to be completed. **Between 1 and 1,000**—Determine specifically how many objectives need to be completed by one gamer or a team to win a match.
Collect Items to End	Based on Items you place on the island while creating it, and items generated by the Item Spawner(s) that you add to your island (also during the building phase), this option allows you to determine how many of those items a gamer or team needs to collect to be declared the winner.	**Off**—Collecting items, such as golden Fortnite Coins or illuminated Pyramids, has no impact on winning the match. **Between 1 and 1,000**—Determine specifically how many items need to be collected by one gamer or a team to win a match.
Score to End	The match can be set up to end once a gamer or team achieves a specific score that you pre-determine.	**Off**—Scoring points has no impact on winning the match. **Between 1 and 1,000**—Determine how many points need to be collected by one gamer or a team to win a match.

MENU OPTION	DESCRIPTION	SETTING OPTIONS
Last Standing	A match ends when only one gamer or team remains alive on the island. This option allows you to replicate the primary objective when playing a Solo, Duos, or Squads match in *Fortnite: Battle Royale*.	**Off**—Becoming the last soldier or team standing on the island has no impact on winning, because your rules of engagement require other objectives to be completed. **On**—The match ends when only one gamer or one team remains alive and all others have been eliminated.
Join in Progress	Determine in advance what happens if a gamer tries to join a match that's already in progress.	**Spectate**—They can watch the match using Spectator mode. **Spawn**—Their soldier can spawn into the match using a Player Spawn that you add to your island during the design and building phase. (Or a soldier will drop from the Battle Bus and freefall to the island if no Player Spawner tiles have been built.)
Spawn Location	Based on the design of your island, you determine exactly where gamers will spawn.	**Spawn Pads**—Gamers can only spawn onto the island using a Player Spawner tile that you've placed while designing the island. Spawn Pads can be pre-programmed so they're team specific. **Sky**—Soldiers entering or re-entering the match will freefall from the Battle Bus. **Current Location**—Soldiers re-spawn at their last location on the map.
Post-Game Spawn Location	Determine where soldiers wind up after a match.	**Island Start**—The location where they started the match. **Pre-Game Location**—This is the location each gamer is placed before the match. This could be the Hub.

MENU OPTION	DESCRIPTION	SETTING OPTIONS
Autostart	Once a Creative map is published, this option determines when the match will begin once all gamers are present.	**Off**—The match must be manually started. **Timer**—The match will automatically begin after 30 seconds, 60 seconds, or 90 seconds.
Vehicle Trick Score Multiplier	If you add drivable vehicles to your island, this option determines the trick score multiplier used when gamers perform tricks while driving a vehicle during a match.	**0.0**—No bonus score multiplier. **Multiplier**—Choose between a 0.1 and 1.9 score multiplier.
Allow Out of Bounds	When you've created an arena or specific area where soldiers can roam on the island, this option can prevent them from leaving that area.	**On**—Players can leave the designated area of the island where a match is supposed to take place (such as within an arena). **Off**—Soldiers must stay within the designated area of the island during a match.
Allow Spectating Other Teams	Once a gamer is eliminated from a match, determine in advance whether they can spectate just members of their own team, or watch the rest of the match from the point of view of opposing team members as well.	**Yes**—Eliminated gamers can spectate and watch the remaining match from any surviving soldier's perspective. **No**—Eliminated gamers can only spectate and watch the match from one of their teammates' perspectives.
Elimination Score	Determine how many points a gamer receives as a result of eliminating another soldier from the match.	Choose between zero and 10,000 points per elimination. Keep in mind, you can also penalize soldiers for causing eliminations and deduct between 1 and 10,000 points per elimination.

The Game Settings Menu

Here's a summary of what each of the options available from the Game Settings submenu are used for when customizing the environment of the island prior to each match.

MENU OPTION	DESCRIPTION	SETTING OPTIONS
Time of Day	Choose the time of day (or night) that the match will begin. This impacts the lighting and what participants will be able to see.	Choose between the Default setting, Random, or select a specific time from the menu.
Light Brightness	Determine the intensity of the sun or how much light the moon generates at night.	Choose between the Default setting or set an intensity percentage (between 10 and 100 percent).
Light Color	Set the tint color of the sun and moon lighting.	Choose between Default, White, Red, Green, Blue, Yellow, Magenta, or Cyan.
Fog Thickness	Decide whether or not you want fog to appear on your island, and if so, how thick it'll be. Fog thickness determines visibility.	Choose between the Default setting and 100 percent (extremely heavy fog).
Fog Color	Choose the color tint that'll be used to display the fog on your island.	Choose between Default, Black, White, Red, Green, Blue, Yellow, Magenta, or Cyan.
Starting Health	A soldier's Health is typically at 100 percent at the start of a Solo, Duos, or Squads match when playing *Fortnite: Battle Royale*, but you can set each soldier's starting Health.	You can make all soldiers Invincible (they can't be harmed during a match) or set their starting Health at 1%, 50% or 100%.

MENU OPTION	DESCRIPTION	SETTING OPTIONS
Max Health	When playing *Fortnite: Battle Royale*, a soldier's Health meter maxes out at 100%. In Creative mode, determine how strong each soldier's Health meter can become.	Choose between 1HP, 25HP, 50HP, 75HP, 100HP, 200HP, 500HP, 1,000HP, 2,000HP, or 10,000HP as a soldier's maximum Health during a match.
Starting Shields	When playing *Fortnite: Battle Royale*, a soldier's Shield meter typically starts at zero, and must be activated and boosted (then replenished) using Shield items. In Creative mode, you can set each soldier's starting Shields level.	Choose between 0%, 50%, or 100%.
Max Shields	When playing *Fortnite: Battle Royale*, a soldier's Shield meter typically maxes out at 100. In Creative mode, you can set each soldier's maximum Shields level.	Choose between No Shields, 25, 50, 75, 100, 200, 500, 1,000, 2,000, or 10,000.
Infinite Ammo	Decide whether or not soldiers will be able to find and collect ammo for their weapons, or if they'll have infinite ammo at their disposal during each match on your island.	**Off**—Soldiers will need to find and collect the five types of ammo. **On**—Unlimited ammo is granted to all soldiers.
Infinite Resources	Normally soldiers need to collect wood, stone, and metal during a match in order to build. You can give them unlimited resources, however.	**On**—All gamers have unlimited wood, stone, and metal for building. **Off**—Soldiers need to find and collect resources in order to build during a match.
Maximum Building Resources	During a typical *Fortnite: Battle Royale* match, a soldier can collect and store a maximum of 1,000 wood, 1,000 stone, and 1,000 metal. In Creative mode, you can change this limit.	Choose between a maximum of zero and 2,000 wood, stone, and metal that can be stored by each soldier during a match.
Harvest Style	Choose the amount of resources a soldier can collect from harvesting wood, stone, or metal using their Harvesting Tool during a match.	Limits are based on Battle Royale, Save the World, or Creative game play mode limits.
Harvest Multiplier	Speed up a soldier's ability to harvest wood, stone, and metal using their Harvesting Tool.	Choose between 0x, 0.1x, 0.5x, 1x, 2x, 3x, 4x, 5x, or 10x.

MENU OPTION	DESCRIPTION	SETTING OPTIONS
Allow Building	Once you've designed your own island, determine whether or not soldiers will be allowed to build (using wood, stone, or metal tiles) during matches.	**On**—Building is allowed. **Off**—No building is allowed.
Building Can Destroy Environment	This option allows you to determine if soldiers who build during a match can alter the environment and potentially destroy pre-created buildings and structures.	**Yes**—Building during a match can destroy and alter pre-existing buildings and structures. **No**—Building during a match can not destroy or alter pre-existing buildings and structures.
Environment Damage	Using weapons and explosives, it's possible to destroy most solid objects (including buildings and structures) when playing *Fortnite: Battle Royale*. You can determine whether or not this is possible during matches that take place on your island.	**On**—Damage and destruction of buildings and structures is possible. **Off**—Damage and destruction of buildings and structures is not possible.
Pickaxe Building Damage	Determine whether or not a soldier's Harvesting Tool can be used to destroy buildings, structures and solid objects—and if so, how long the destruction will take.	Choose between Instant, None, and Default.
Down But Not Out	Decide whether gamers can be healed by teammates during a match.	Choose between Default, On, or Off.
Keep Items When Eliminated	If soldiers can be respawned during a match, determine if they'll keep their weapons and items each time they re-enter the match.	**Keep**—Soldiers will keep everything they had in their inventory. **Delete**—Items soldiers had will be lost. **Drop**—Items from the soldier's inventory will respawn near the soldier's respawn location.
Allow Items to Be Dropped	Determine whether or not a soldier can drop (and potentially share) items from their inventory during a game.	**Yes**—Dropping is allowed. **No**—Dropping is not allowed.

MENU OPTION	DESCRIPTION	SETTING OPTIONS
Allow Item Pick Up	Choose whether or not items can be picked up and added to a soldier's inventory during a match.	**Yes**—Items can be picked up. **No**—Items cannot be picked up.
Respawn Time	Set how long an eliminated soldier will need to wait before respawning back into the match.	Choose between one second and 30 seconds.
Spawn Immunity Item	Determine how long a soldier will be invincible to attacks after re-entering a match.	Choose between zero and 10 minutes.
Fall Damage	Decide whether or not a soldier can receive damage from a fall during a match.	**Yes**—Fall damage is possible. **No**—Fall damage is not possible.
Gravity	Set the entire island's gravity level. This will apply to all soldiers on the island.	Choose between Normal, High, Very High, Very Low, or Low
Jump Fatigue	Turning on this feature will cause a soldier to get tired after multiple jumps. Rest will be required before performing additional jumps.	**On**—A soldier will get tired after a few jumps. **Off**—Unlimited jumping is possible, with no fatigue caused.
Glider Redeploy	Without using a Glider Item, determine if a soldier can redeploy their Glider during a match when leaping (or falling) from high places.	**On**—The Glider can be used. **Off**—The Glider cannot be redeployed without using a Glider item.
Player Flight	Allow soldiers to fly around the island (as opposed to walking, running, jumping, driving in a vehicle, or using Balloons, for example).	**On**—Flying is allowed by double-tapping the Jump button. **Off**—No flying is allowed.
Player Flight Sprint	If flying is allowed, a soldier's flight speed can be increased by sprinting.	**On**—Faster flight is possible. **Off**—Faster flight is not possible.
Flight Speed	Set the maximum flight speed, if flying is allowed.	Choose between 0x and 3.0X.
Player Names and Locations	Determine what information about gamers will be displayed to everyone, versus what only team members will see during a match.	Choose between Team Only, Always Show, and Always Hide
Health Granted on Elimination	Decide whether a soldier will receive bonus Health replenishment if they eliminate an enemy.	Choose between zero and 1,000 Health HP, based on the maximum Health meter capacity you've previously selected.

MENU OPTION	DESCRIPTION	SETTING OPTIONS
Wood, Stone, and Metal Granted on Elimination	Separately determine if a soldier will receive bonus wood, stone, or metal each time they eliminate an enemy from the match.	Choose between 0 and 999 of each resource.
Damage Select on Hit Amount	Determine whether a gamer can injure their own soldier if the soldier hits something.	Determine the level of damage a soldier can inflict upon themselves.
Damage Self-Target Filter	Set what types of targets can cause self-damage to a soldier if they get hit.	Choose between All, Non-Players, and Players Only
Damage Self-Weapon Filter	Decide whether or not a soldier can injure themselves using their own weapons. If you permit this, select the type(s) of weapons that can cause injury.	Choose between Pickaxe Only, Melee Only, Ranged Only, or All Weapons.
Allow Manual Respawning	Determine whether or not players can manually respawn during a match by selecting the Respawn option from the game Menu.	**Yes**—Manual respawning anytime during a match is possible. **No**—Manual respawning is not possible.

The UI (User Interface) Settings Menu

Here's a summary of what each of the options available from the UI Settings submenu are used for when it comes to customizing your island. These options relate to the user interface and what gamers will see on their screen during each match that takes place on your island.

MENU OPTION	DESCRIPTION	SETTING OPTIONS
Time	If you've added a mini-game timer to the island (from the Devices submenu when designing your island) this option determines whether the timer counts up or down.	Choose between Count Down or Count Up.
Game Winner Time Displayed	Determine how long the winner's name appears on the screen at the end of a match.	Choose Don't Show or between three and 30 seconds.
Game Score Display Time	Determine how long the match scoreboard will be displayed at the end of a match.	Choose Don't Show or between three and 30 seconds.
Round Winner Display Time	If your match includes Rounds, determine how long the winner's name will be displayed at the end of each Round.	Choose Don't Show or between three and 30 seconds.
Round Score Display Time	If your match includes Rounds, determine how long the scoreboard will be displayed at the end of each Round.	Choose Don't Show or between three and 30 seconds.
HUD Type	Select the Heads Up Display type that will be displayed for gamers during each match.	Options include: Default, Creature Elimination, Score, or Objectives.
Scoreboard Win Condition	Set what is required for a gamer to win.	Options include: None, Eliminations, Assists, Eliminated, Collect Items, Health, Creatures, Score, Objective, Time, or Spawns Left.
Scoreboard Tiebreaker #1, #2, #3, and #4	Set up to four different tiebreaker conditions.	Options include: None, Eliminations, Assists, Eliminated, Collect Items, Health, Creatures, Score, Objectives, Time, or Spawns Left.
Map Display Widget	Decide what information, along with or instead of the Island Map will be displayed when a gamer accesses the Map screen during a match.	Options include: Scoreboard or Default Map

MENU OPTION	DESCRIPTION	SETTING OPTIONS
Show Island Code Watermark	Each time you publish an island map, it's given a unique ID number. Instead of displaying the compass near the top-center of the game screen during a match, the island's number and the creator's name can be displayed.	**On**—The Creator's name and the map ID number is displayed instead of the compass during a match. **Off**—Just the compass is displayed.

The Island Tools Menu

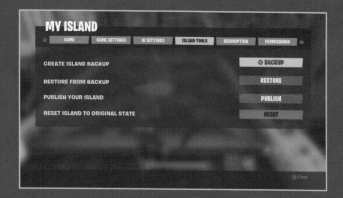

Here's a summary of how each of the options available from the Island Tools submenu are used. This menu has three main options—Backup, Restore, and Reset (Delete).

Anytime you're investing significant time designing and creating an island map from scratch using Creative mode, periodically access the Island Tools submenu and use the Backup option to create a backup of your work. Should something happen that results in your work getting lost, corrupted, or accidently erased, use the Restore button to reload your work from the backup file.

If you want to delete a map you've created, select the Reset option and then use the Confirm command to remove everything from the island and restore it to its original state. There is a limit to how many island maps your Epic Games account can store. To make room for new maps, you may occasionally need to delete old ones.

The Description Menu

If you plan to publish your island and make it available to friends or the general Fortnite gaming public, it's important to give your island a unique name and description, plus add to the description details about the unique rules of engagement you've established. All of this is done from the Description submenu.

Within the Title field, use up to 40 characters to give your island a unique, attention-grabbing, and descriptive title. Be creative and brainstorm a title that'll make gamers want to check out your island!

Use the Description field to create a one-sentence (up to 150 character) description of your island and its rules of engagement. You can add additional lines to your island's description (each can be up to 150 characters long) using the Add Another Bullet command. Use the description to describe the island itself, whether it's a solo or team-oriented challenge, and what the main rules of engagement (as well as the match's objectives) are.

If you're not sure what information to include in your island's description, check out the descriptions of other gamer-created island maps for some ideas. However, it's important to make your title and descriptions as unique as possible.

Especially if you've become part of the Support A Creator program and will be making your island maps available to the public, including detailed descriptions is important if you want gamers to try out and enjoy your maps. Within the description, include the match objectives, rules, and any other information that won't be obvious to a gamer. One of the biggest mistakes map creators make is designing incredible maps and then not properly explaining the best way to experience them.

Once you've used your keyboard (or the virtual on-screen keyboard) to fill in the Title and Description fields, be sure to use the Apply command to save your changes. If you want to erase the information you've already entered into these fields and start again, use the Clear All command. This only deletes the text from the Title and Description fields, not the data related to your actual island map.

Another way to present the rules of engagement for your island to gamers is to add one or more Billboards (from the Devices menu) that will be visible when a match begins and gamers get transported to your island.

You're able to add custom text to each Billboard using the Billboard customization tools offered within Creative mode. Refer back to the **Master Combat Series Demo Deathrun** map (Map Code: 7165-8631-4334) to see an example of how Billboards can be used at the start of a match.

The Permissions Menu

This submenu only has one option to customize. It's labeled Island Edit Permission. Decide whether your island will be private or if everyone who uses it will be able to edit it. Choose between these two options and then use the Apply command to save your changes.

Assuming you've created something amazing, you might want to get your island listed on some of the independent websites that maintain a database of island maps created by gamers using Creative mode. Several of these sites are listed within **Section 4— Fortnite: Creative Resources**.

How to Publish Your Creative Maps Online

As of fall 2019, there are two ways to publish your island maps publicly, although additional options may become available in the future. First, submit your creation directly to Epic Games to possibly be a Featured Island within the game or in The Block. The other option is to join the Support A Creator program, which allows you to publish your map codes publicly.

Within *Fortnite: Battle Royale*, on the island map is a point of interest called The Block. Within this area, Epic Games is able to "drop in" island maps created by gamers using *Fortnite: Creative* that are submitted for temporary inclusion within the game.

If you choose to submit your island to be considered for inclusion within The Block, it must meet very specific requirements. For example, it can only be 25 tiles by 25 tiles large. To read up on the special requirements for maps to be included within The Block, visit: www.epicgames.com/fortnite/en-US/news/the-block.

Submit Your Maps Directly to Epic Games

Submit your map directly to Epic Games for consideration and invite the company to showcase your work within the game—either as a Featured Island or within The Block. Realistically, they get thousands of submissions per week, but only feature a few per day, so unless you've created something totally lit and extremely original, the chances of your map getting noticed by the folks at Epic Games are rather slim.

Once your map is completed and ready to be experienced, if you want to submit it to Epic Games, visit this website and follow the instructions carefully—www.epicgames.com/fortnite/en-US/news/creative-featured-content.

On the Creative Featured Content webpage, look for the sentence that says, "Click here to head to the official content submission page. On this page, you can submit your block or featured island creations." Click on the hyperlink and complete the entire form before submitting it.

As you'll discover, there are very specific Featured Island and Block guidelines that must be met in order for Epic Games to feature it.

Epic Games also recommends gamers planning to submit their map(s) for consideration join the Official Creator Discord. You can sign up for free by visiting this website: https://discord.gg/8hpRSSM.

How to Join the Support A Creator Program

As of fall 2019, if you want to share your maps with the public and have each map assigned its own 12-digit Island Map Code (which you can promote), you'll first need to join Epic's Support A Creator program.

To join the Support A Creator program, you must have at least 1,000 followers on at least one social media platform, such as Instagram, Twitter, YouTube, Twitch.tv, or Facebook. The application process for this program takes about 15 minutes to complete, and the approval process can take anywhere from a few hours to a few weeks, so be patient.

Once you're accepted into the program, you can earn money by having your social media followers "support" you when they play *Fortnite*. You're also able to generate Island Map Codes that can be published anywhere, allowing gamers to access and experience the maps you create using *Fortnite: Creative*.

To learn more about the Support A Creator program, visit: www.epicgames.com/affiliate/en-US/overview.

Your unique Island Map Code is displayed within seconds after you publish a map. You can now share this code with your online friends or the general gaming public. Make sure your island is 100 percent completed and fully functional before publishing it. If you need to make changes to your island after it's been published, it will receive a new code.

Once you're accepted into the Support A Creator program, you can publish your island maps. Click on the Publish icon and your map will be assigned its own 12-digit Island Map Code.

Any Fortniter can then access the Creative Hub, approach a Rift, choose the Change Destination option, enter your Island Map Code, and once the map loads, walk into the Rift. If it's a multiplayer map, be sure to invite at least one friend to join your party, so you have someone to compete against before walking through the Rift.

After entering an Island Map Code and walking into its Rift, the gamer simply needs to click on the Start Game button to begin the match, unless it's set to auto-start.

How to Experience Your Creative Maps with Online Friends

Once you've created your custom map, the next step is to invite your friends to join matches that'll take place on your island.

From the Creative Lobby, select the Online Friends icon displayed in the top-left corner of the screen, or press the Menu button.

As you're viewing your list of online friends, one at a time, select a friend's listing. Here, RustyTheYorkie was first invited to become an online friend. The invitation from JasonRich7 was accepted.

Select one online friend at a time and use the Join Party option to invite each gamer to join a match on your island.

From back at the Lobby, wait for the newly invited friend to join the party, and then select the Play option to begin the match.

If your Creative Map is loaded and open within your account, and you're online, your online friends should see a listing for your map on the Select A Server screen. They can then request to join the party.

Discover What It Takes to Create an Amazing Map

Out of all the gamers who publish maps using *Fortnite: Creative*, a few stand out for their superior work. Jesper Gran (known online as Jesgran) has published several of what have become extremely popular maps. In addition to YouTube, you'll find Jesgran on Instagram (www.instagram.com/jesleaks) and on Reddit (www.reddit.com/user/jespergran).

Here is info about three of his creations:

Jesgran's Deathrun 2.0 (Map Code: 1103-0256-3362) is a popular deathrun map. Check out the animated trailer for this map on YouTube (https://youtu.be/b-uWR5PUQ9M). The goal of every deathrun map is to challenge gamers to race through the map, as quickly as possible, without being eliminated by the traps, obstacles, and enemies that are placed in their path.

Jesgran's Deathrun 3.0 (Map Code: 4893-9258-8488) is another extremely popular deathrun map that offers a different visual design and a whole new set of challenges. Check out the animated trailer for this map on YouTube (https://youtu.be/nqj-_LztuhU).

Sky Royale (Map Code: 4151-6253-9143) is a two to 16 player mini-game that includes plenty of battle royale-style combat. The animated trailer for this popular map can be watched on YouTube (https://youtu.be/lWZpD0Ogdw0).

Six Map Creation Tips from Jesgran

Jesgran will often spend hundreds of hours creating a single map using *Fortnite: Creative* in order to publish a map that's challenging, visually interesting, unique, and fun to play. He offers these six tips to first-time map creators:

- **Tip #1**—Be patient during the creative process. You can't make a good map in only a few hours.
- **Tip #2**—To get inspiration for new map ideas, look at posts on social media, as well as the Creative forum on Reddit (www.reddit.com/r/FortniteCreative), and check out the daily Creative maps featured within the game itself.
- **Tip #3**—From a creative standpoint, remember that you can always rescale and rotate props so they don't look copied when you use many of them. Doing this will give your map a more organic look, as opposed to a copy and pasted look.
- **Tip #4**—Try to use as few Prefabs as possible. If you want to use a Prefab, use it in a smart way, so it takes longer for you to reach the one hundred thousand memory unit maximum. A single prop or Prefab can take over 1,000 memory if you only have one of it on your map.
- **Tip #5**—Focus evenly on level design and visual design. You don't want to decorate too much, and make the game play too hard, misleading, or confusing for players. At the same time, you don't want your map to look too generic. Level design relates to the challenges and difficulty level you build into the map. In other words, what players will need to accomplish. Visual design focuses exclusively on how the map looks.
- **Tip #6**—Instead of focusing on creating very large buildings or structures from scratch, which can get very complicated, focus on making really good looking and well-decorated smaller buildings or structures instead.

Let's Create a Sample Island

Now that you understand the steps involved with designing, creating, publishing (saving), and experiencing an island created using Creative mode, let's take a look at a sample island being created. You can access this sample map yourself using Map Code: 3343-4059-4532.

This sample map is called Master Combat Sample Island. It was created on the Artic Island 1 terrain map, and it's a two-team death match that features four Rounds, during which the goal is to acquire 30 Eliminations to win. Between two and 10 gamers can experience each match.

The main structures on the map include two Paradise Palm Hotels. The entire arena had been surrounded by walls. While gamers can have their soldiers leave the arena during a match, there's really no purpose to exiting the hotel grounds.

Many walls, floors, and ceiling tiles from the Paradise Palms Gallery were used to customize the layout of the hotels and create the rest of the fighting arena.

Located throughout the arena are several Item/Weapon Spawner tiles. Everything you find on one side of the arena has been mirrored on the opposite side, so the two teams will be evenly matched in terms of what's available to them.

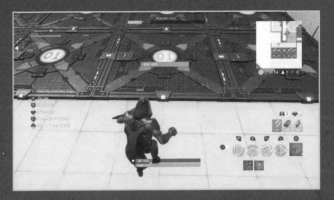

Player Spawner and Item Spawner tiles have been placed together for each team, so at the start of a match, team members begin at the same place and can quickly grab weapons.

The Weapon Spawner tiles have been placed in a separate area from the Heath/Shield-related Spawner tiles, which forces the soldiers to move around within the map to fully build up their arsenal and then boost their Health and Shield meters.

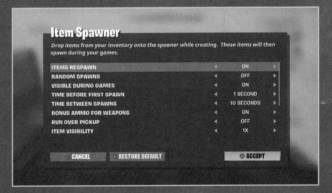

The Item Spawners have each been customized separately.

During a match, the Item Spawners that spew out Health and Shield replenishment items can be found on ground level (shown here), as well as near the platforms built onto the roofs of the hotels. Memorize their locations so you can easily get back to them anytime your soldier needs to replenish their Health or Shield meter after a firefight or attack.

From the Team Select window, each player will need to choose a Team. For example, if just two gamers are playing, one person should choose Team 1 and the other should choose Team 2. Once a team has been chosen, exit the menu and press the Start Game option from the map's title screen.

At the start of each match, the spawn location for each gamer will depend on which team they've chosen to join. Surrounding the soldiers on both teams are five different Weapon Spawner tiles.

Each Weapon Spawner tile generates a random weapon in a specific category, so if you're short on time and need to grab the most powerful weapon possible, head directly to the Weapon Spawner that's churning out Legendary (gold) weapons.

When you play a team-oriented match to be experienced on a map created using Fortnite: Creative, before pressing the Start Game button to kick off the match, it's often necessary for each player to manually choose their team. This is necessary when playing matches on the Master Combat Sample Island map. From the map's title screen, press the Menu button on your keyboard or controller. From the menu on the right side of the screen (shown here), choose the Team Select option.

Scattered throughout the open areas of this map are a bunch of smaller walls and objects that can be used by soldiers to hide behind or climb up on. The design of this map focuses on both close- and long-range combat, so there are also plenty of high locations a soldier can reach in order to gain a height advantage on their enemies.

To get over high walls and quickly reach other areas of the map, be sure to climb up on objects and hedges, for example.

To ensure this island requires some exploration, in addition to combat, it's designed so soldiers will need to go inside of buildings, position themselves at high places (shown here), plus navigate around at ground level in order to build their arsenal, stay safe, and find locations from which to launch attacks that have a tactical advantage.

Getting your soldier high up and using a Sniper Rifle (or any weapon with a scope) will allow you to pick off your enemies from a distance.

While inside either of the hotels, close range combat will become necessary, especially if you're playing against several other gamers.

While you'll be able to expand your soldier's arsenal by returning to the Weapon Spawner tiles, reaching these locations will force your soldier out in the open, where they're highly vulnerable to attack—especially from above. On the plus side, each time you grab a weapon, you'll receive a very generous supply ammo.

During matches that take place on this Master Combat Sample Island map, it is not possible to destroy any of the structures using the Harvesting Tool, weapons, or explosives. Building has also been disabled, so you'll need to rely on the terrain that surrounds your soldier in order to remain safe. The explosion shown here caused zero damage to the staircase or building.

Located on top of both hotels are custom-created platforms that allow soldiers to reach even higher points so they can gain a height advantage during combat. While your soldier is on one of the platforms, be on the lookout for Item Spawner tiles that generate useful Health items, including Small Shield Potions and Slurp Juice.

Throughout this map, fall damage has been activated, but the use of the Glider has been deactivated. Leaping from high floors of the hotel to get back to ground level is definitely not a good idea.

Now that you have an idea of what the **Master Combat Sample Map** looks like during a match, take a look at the My Island menu screens used to customize matches being played on this map.

The Master Combat Sample Map Game menu screen.

The Master Combat Sample Map Game Settings menu screen.

The Master Combat Sample Map UI Setting menu screen.

SECTION 3

DISCOVER WHAT OTHER *FORTNITE* EXPERTS HAVE CREATED

The game developers at Epic Games are basically geniuses when it comes to creating and updating *Fortnite: Battle Royale* in a way that keeps the game exciting, challenging, and fun to play. By offering Fortniters the Creative toolbox, fans can create their own island maps and matches from scratch, without having to do any programming whatsoever.

Since *Fortnite: Creative* was released, thousands of island maps have been created, and many have been published and made public.

Keep in mind, *Fortnite: Creative* can be a bit glitchy. This is *not* the fault of the map creators. There may be times when you need to return to the Hub or exit out of Creative mode altogether, and then re-enter the map you want to experience in order for it to work properly. With each major game update, the folks at Epic Games continue to make dramatic improvements to *Fortnite: Creative*.

This section showcases more than 25 awesome, original, and unique island maps that are available to the public.

How to Access a Creative Map

To access any of these *Fortnite: Creative* maps, follow these steps:

Step #1 - Either from the main menu or from the Game Play Mode selection menu, select Creative.

Step #2–From the Lobby (or the Creative Hub), if you want to invite online friends to participate in a match to take place on a Creative island, access the Menu. From the Friends menu (on the left side of the screen) invite one gamer at a time to your party.

Step #3—When everyone in your party is present in the Lobby, choose the Play option.

Step #4—Scroll to the extreme right of the Select A Server screen and select Launch in conjunction with the Start A Server option.

Step #5—Your soldier's next stop is the Hub. Walk up the stairs to the right or left of where your soldier is facing.

Step #6—Walk up to any Featured Creation portal, but do not walk through the Rift. Instead, press the keyboard key or mouse button that corresponds with the Change Destination option. On a PS4, press the controller's Square button. If you're playing on a Windows PC, press the "E" key.

Step #7—When the Island Codes screen appears, use the keyboard to delete the 12-digit code that's currently displayed, and manually enter the 12-digit code for the map you want to access. You do not need to include the dashes. Select the Done button to continue.

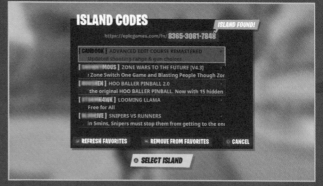

Step #8—Assuming you entered a valid map code, the "Island Found" banner will appear in the top-right corner of the Island Codes window. Click on the Select Island button (near the bottom-center of the screen) to load the map.

Map Title:	Advanced Edit Course (Remastered)
Island Code:	8365-3081-7848
Creator:	CanDook
Creator's YouTube Channel:	www.youtube.com/channel/ UCLafGPLC9pXgDQqIVpDMpzw

Step #9—Your soldier will be transported back to the Hub. It may take between 30 and 60 seconds for the map to load. When it does, the title of the map will appear above the Rift. Have your soldier walk into the Rift to be transported to the island. All soldiers participating in the match should enter the same Rift.

This map offers an intricate maze. To reach the end, you'll need to practice your editing skills in building mode, use your soldier's Harvesting Tool to smash through walls and building tiles, plus do a whole lot of exploring.

Step #10—The title screen for the map you selected will be displayed. Click the Start Game button to begin the match.

Each match only lasts 10 minutes, so you'd better hurry.

25 *Fortnite: Creative* Maps That Are Worth Checking Out

The maps showcased in this section are listed alphabetically by the map's title, not in order of their popularity. Most are shown here being played on a Windows 10 PC, although each can be played on any compatible gaming system.

Be ready to climb past obstacles, smash your way through them using your soldier's Harvesting Tool, or use the Edit functions while in Building mode to create openings your soldier can walk or crouch through.

Some of the pathways require your soldier to leap from platform to platform as they make their way upwards.

Along the way, you'll discover a few weapons that'll you'll need to use to shoot at specific targets in order to proceed. Use the mini-map to help you navigate around the map. You are allowed to build. Falling out of the maze arena, however, will result in your soldier's demise.

This is one of the shooting ranges you'll discover as you explore this map.

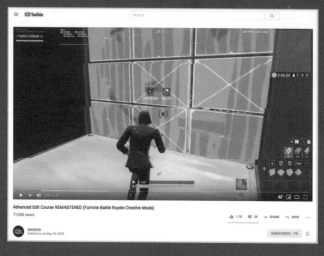

Check out the animated trailer for this map on YouTube (www. youtube.com/watch?v=InjMVAT_R78).

Map Title:	Cizzorz Deathrun 3.0
Island Code:	4043-5793-6999
Creator:	ITSCIZZORZ
Creator's YouTube Channel:	www.youtube.com/user/Cizzorz

This deathrun map is chock full of solo challenges that require you to use items and weapons to get past certain obstacles. During your trek through the map, be sure to collect golden Fortnite coins. The map contains 16 levels that become exceedingly more difficult as you progress.

As a result of the incredible popularity of this map, several YouTubers have published cheat videos that'll help you proceed through some of the more challenging levels. For example, check out this video from JDuth (www.youtube.com/watch?v=emuWdR3ykAM).

Things are not always as they seem when playing this deathrun map. At the very start, the Level 1 doorway may seem like the path you want to take, but don't be fooled! It's not.

Instead, follow the path to the left that leads to the Trap on the ground and jump down through the Trap. This Trap is just an illusion. You'll drop to a lower level that'll lead you to toward the real Checkpoint #1.

After falling through the Trap in the floor, follow the hallway to the right or left and look for the actual start of this deathrun.

Run over the Ice Block so your soldier's feet turn into ice blocks, allowing them to slide through the next areas of the map. Jump over the pits that contain real Traps, but make sure you stay in control so you don't crash into a Trap on a wall and perish.

This deathrun is as much about perfect timing as it is about problem solving and using the items and tools you come across in creative ways.

Map Title:	Crab Rave
Island Code:	8552-3258-2013
Creator:	Roeloffsyt
Creator's YouTube Channel:	www.youtube.com/user/ SlyzeNL

So there's not really a challenge in this map, but its creator has expertly used music blocks (which are a building tool incorporated into *Fortnite: Creative*).

Once the map is loaded, have your soldier run, not walk, through the maze—directly over the multi-colored music blocks. You'll hear the popular Crab Rave tune.

There are two colorful pathways to follow on this map as you enjoy the musical accompaniment.

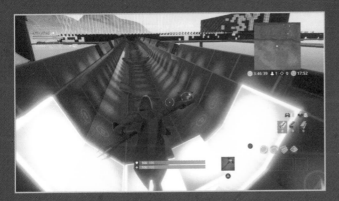

If you're impressed by this, be sure to check out Meme Island (Including Crab Rave 2.0) by Reoloffsyt using Island Map Code: 6076-7447-1769. This multi-player map contains five distinct areas to run or drive through, each of which generates a different music track.

Check out the animated trailer for this map on YouTube (www.youtube.com/watch?v=6kfqycH1AjE).

Map Title:	Dead By Fortlight II
Island Code:	3081-6247-3631
Creator:	thyrosx
Creator's YouTube Channel:	www.youtube.com/channel/UCX8TIM9T03iq9lwRRbtHwTQ

This is an original map with a storyline. The goal is to explore the otherworld, find and disable all five generators, and get transported back to your own world after saving your soul. If you experience just one of the maps featured in this guide, Dead by Fortlight II should be the one you select!

Dead by Fortlight II takes place in a graveyard and massive stone castle setting that's surrounded by lava. Matches don't involve combat. This map offers more of a seek and destroy mission with no time limit. From a visual and originality standpoint, this map is truly stunning!

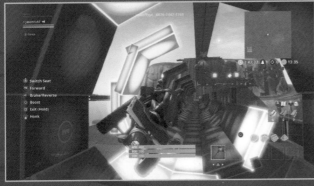

Not only does this sequel map offer more musical routes to follow, you can also drive along the multi-colored musical pathways using a Baller or Quadcrasher. The trick is to discover the best travel speed so the music's tempo sounds perfect.

At the start of this match, be sure to switch teams and select Team 2.

The storm has arrived, but in this scenario, it's not deadly. The lava pools, however, do pose a Health threat.

Your first objective is to grab the Infinity Blade.

There are many structures to explore, most of which are empty. Because of the darkness, it's hard to keep from getting lost or traveling around in circles.

If you accomplish the map's objective, a portal will unlock and your soldier will be able to grab a coin to win. This detailed map was designed for between one and 16 gamers.

Try and keep track of where you've been as you seek out and then deactivate each of the five generators.

Check out the animated trailer for this map on YouTube (www.youtube.com/watch?v=cT9S6BUkjiA).

for this map on YouTube (www.youtube.com/watch?v=sw2qH12_brY).

One of the mini-games, called ATK Sumo, involves a multi-player ATK bumper car challenge that takes place on an elevated platform.

Map Title:	Fortnite Arcade
Island Code:	2900-4196-3823
Creator:	OmegaNovaToo
Creator's YouTube Channel:	www.youtube.com/channel/UC_dKD9Ay4yTGLpx1GTqNy9A

This one map offers a new twist to seven popular arcade and theme park adventures by allowing gamers to participate in a series of mini-games and obstacle course challenges. Be sure to watch the animated trailer

The goal is to knock the other ATKs off the platform, without accidently driving or being knocked off of the platform by someone else. It's best to nudge your ATK forward by tapping on the gas pedal, as opposed to holding it down. If you pick up too much speed, you won't be able to stop or turn fast enough to avoid driving off of the platform.

In the Duck Hunt mini-game, you'll need to open a chest, grab some scoped weapons, and then shoot at enemies on the opposite side of the arena.

As the runners go back and forth across the structure while playing Duck Hunt, they'll encounter multiple obstacles on each level. The staircase to get up a level is always on the opposite side from where they just entered the level. Don't forget, if you're a runner, the Sniper will be trying to track your movements and shoot at you from afar.

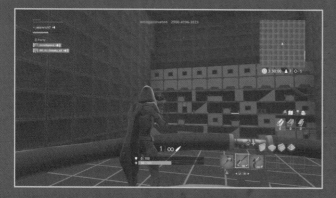

The ATK Race offers a multi-level, rather intricate track that you can race along alone (against the clock) or test your driving skills against other gamers. Blue arrows on the walls show you the route.

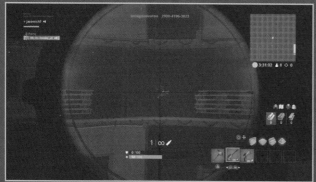

One player is the shooter. He stands on a platform on the opposite side of the arena and uses a scoped weapon to try to target the runners who must go back and forth as they make their way up the structure.

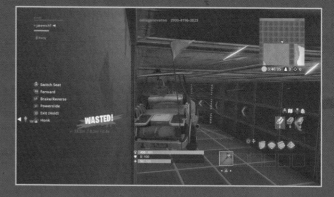

Since you can't use an ATK's Turbo feature, you'll need to use the Speed Boost and Movement Modulator tiles on the track, as well as your navigational skills to achieve speed, potentially go airborne, and reach the Finish Line as quickly as possible without accidently flipping your ATK (which wastes valuable time).

Grapple Arena is a multi-level obstacle course that requires the skillful use of a Grappler to get around.

There are multiple entrances into Grapple Arena, and some make it easier to survive in this area than others.

Don't forget to grab a Grappler from a chest before entering the area. Each Grappler offers an infinite number of shots when experiencing this map, so don't worry about conserving shots. Use as many as you need to avoid crashing to the ground and being eliminated.

Map Title:	Fury Racing—Snowy Summit
Island Code:	1731-2660-6859
Creator:	axel-capek
Creator's YouTube Channel:	www.youtube.com/watch?v=Fhjr-diZ1_o

This five-minute race puts you in the driver's seat of a Quadcrasher. Your goal is to race around an obstacle course as quickly as possible, while collecting as many golden *Fortnite* coins as you can.

Next, go down the opposite alley and toss the Port-A-Fort onto the target on the floor.

Play alone or against a group of your online friends. You'll need to drive fast, but stay in control, so you can make sharp turns and sudden course changes as needed. If you crash, you'll need to respawn and try again from the starting line.

Return to the Starting Line, jump into a Quadcrasher, and wait for the forcefield to disappear. The countdown timer has already started, but for you, the race has only just begun.

At the start of a race, there's a forcefield across the Starting Line that you won't initially be able to pass through. Before hopping on your Quadcrasher, find and grab a Port-A-Fort.

Follow the arrows and light posts along the sides of the track to help you navigate.

Be sure to collect as many golden Fortnite coins as you can. Collecting multiple coins in a row earns you a point bonus. Sometimes, it's better to proceed along the track at a slower pace, but collect extra coins, as opposed to traveling at top speed and not having enough control to grab the coins and stay on the track.

Stay in control of your vehicle. It's easy to flip it. When your soldier's vehicle flips, have them exit the Quadcrasher, flip the vehicle so it's upright, and then jump back into the driver's seat. This wastes valuable time, so try to avoid flipping the vehicle too often.

Map Title:	Gas Station Prop Hunt
Island Code:	6495-3159-8845 (Day Version) or 8528-2902-4418 (Night Version)
Creator:	CanDook
Creator's YouTube Channel:	www.youtube.com/channel/ UCLafGPLC9pXgDQqIVpDMpzw

This is a Prop Hunt map that requires you to . . . you guessed it . . . hunt Props if you're the Hunter or outsmart the Hunter if you become a Prop. At least two gamers are required to experience this map.

The main map area contains a gas station, parking lot, and supermarket, so it's not too large. However, the map offers plenty of items and objects Props can transform into, so you'll definitely be kept busy and challenged.

Check out the animated trailer for this map on YouTube (www.youtube.com/watch?v =Kyx7GWZekIU).

If your vehicle's HP meter hits zero before you reach the finish line, you'll be eliminated from the race and your soldier's vehicle will explode.

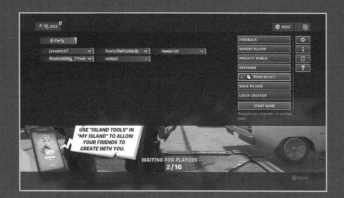

At the start of a match, at least one player needs to switch teams by accessing the menu and choosing the Team Select option.

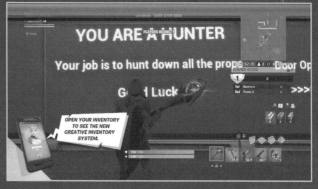

The Hunter will spawn in a large room at the start of the match. After about 30 seconds (while the Props are hiding), a wall will open. When you're the Hunter, as you explore the map, each time you shoot something that isn't a Prop, your soldier's Health meter loses 5HP. When their Health meter hits zero, you're done and the match ends.

A Prop is a soldier that disguises themselves as any object from Fortnite: Battle Royale, who must hide in plain sight and avoid being shot at. As a Prop your soldier is equipped with a Prop-O-Matic gun.

If you shoot something and your soldier's Health meter does not go down, this means you've discovered a Prop. Keep shooting to destroy it and eliminate that player.

Point the Prop-O-Matic at almost any object and your soldier will be transformed into that object. While in disguise, you can move around and even use most emotes, but to avoid detection, it's best to find a place to hide in plain sight and then stay still.

As a Prop, once you find a disguise and hiding spot, don't move or you'll quickly be detected by the Hunter. Props can change their identity as often as they wish, but by doing so, they run the risk of being discovered by the Hunter. Shown here, the Prop has transformed into a grocery store shelf and is moving freely around the store looking for a hiding spot so he blends in with the scenery. When you're a Prop, consider using emotes to taunt the Hunter if they're having trouble spotting you.

Map Title:	Hollywood Movie Studio Prop Hunt
Island Code:	4295-0113-7083
Creator:	BluDrive
Creator's YouTube Channel:	www.youtube.com/channel/UCJ2_fYZTg8okhtDzcflBegg

Welcome to Hollywood, California. A movie studio is the backdrop for this highly creative map that allows multiple gamers to participate in a Prop Hunt.

There's an animated trailer for this map that you can watch on YouTube (www.youtube.com/watch?v=cMkEIi4wZBQ). To watch BluDrive's tutorial on how a Prop Hunt map is created, watch this video (www.youtube.com/watch?v=KtNH6AfO19c).

In any Prop Hunt game, there's a Seeker (also referred to as a Hunter), and the Props. The Props are soldiers controlled by gamers who disguise themselves as almost any item or object from Fortnite: Battle Royale and then hide in plain sight.

As a Prop, once you've found your hiding spot (often in plain sight), use the Toggle Lock-in-Place command to set yourself down at that location. Again, try to find a hiding spot where you blend in. As a payphone, positioning yourself on a canoe in the middle of water is definitely going to get you noticed. Thus, it's a bad idea.

Once a Prop disguises themselves (in this case as a payphone), they can still move around the map and use Emotes. Shown here, the payphone is running down the street, out in the open. The goal, however, is to stand still and blend in with the rest of the island's décor, so not to get detected.

The goal of a Prop is to blend in with their surroundings and avoid being detected and shot at by the Seeker. It's like a game of hide and seek, but with disguises. As a Prop, you need to successfully hide on a movie set for six minutes without being detected in order to win the match. When a Prop is discovered and eliminated by the Seeker, that Prop becomes a Seeker as well.

As a Prop, you're equipped with a Prop-O-Matic gun. Point it at almost any object and your soldier will be transformed into that object. While in disguise, you can move around and even use most emotes, but to avoid detection, it's best to find a place to hide in plain sight and then stay still. To make things a bit more fun, Props can taunt the Seeker and change their appearance as often as they wish during a match.

This Hollywood Movie Studio map is large, extremely detailed, and very well designed, so expect to experience some stellar red carpet battles. The more gamers you play with, the more fun you'll have when experiencing this map. Shown here is the Hunter entering the movie studio. When playing this map, the game automatically assigns players to be either the Hunter or a Prop.

When the Hunter finds and shoots a Prop, the Round ends.

Map Title:	Hoo Baller Pinball 2.0
Island Code:	7783-5002-0010
Creator:	hooshen
Creator's YouTube Channel:	www.youtube.com/hooshen

Transport inside a massive, custom-designed pinball machine, and then have your soldier hop into a Baller to become the pinball as you bounce and roll around. If you enjoy this pinball machine map, check out the original Hoo Baller Pinball map using Map Code: 7164-9264-6925.

This pinball machine map features 15 hidden tunnels. There's no combat taking place on this mega-creative map, but the high-speed pinball game action is non-stop and very nicely designed.

The goal is to be the first to earn 200 points within the allocated five-minute time period. Points are collected by running over small silver orbs that are scattered throughout the pinball arena.

Hop into a Baller at the start of a Round and be prepared to be bounced around.

Driving or bouncing into bumpers, paddles, and other objects within the pinball map will keep your Baller moving, but the ultimate goal is to run over the silver spheres and collect points, so do your best to navigate.

There are ways to be flung out of the Baller during a match. Your soldier can still bounce around and collect points. Without the Baller, in some ways you have more precise control over your soldier's movement, but the experience of actually being the pinball in a pinball machine gets lost, although the speed of the match continues to be intense.

Map Title:	Jduth's 100 Level Default Deathrun
Island Code:	0079-8125-3099
Creator:	Jduth96
Creator's YouTube Channel:	www.youtube.com/ JDuthBasketball

Your objective is to reach all 100 checkpoints as quickly as possible, but avoiding the many traps, obstacles, and surprises intentionally placed in your path. Check out the YouTube video of jduth96 completing his own scenario - www.youtube.com/watch?v=7F9oZMY7_Qc.

Each of the 100 checkpoints is labeled with a giant number. Have your soldier walk or run over the checkpoint pad.

This is a solo, maze-like "deathrun" scenario that requires you to move as quickly as possible through the island. Getting past the first few checkpoints involves running, jumping, and perfect timing.

Sometimes the path ahead will be obvious—that is, until you reach a trap or obstacle that blocks you. With no weapons or resources, one of your first challenges is to get past this trap.

At the start of the match, you'll discover two giant Loot Llamas on either side of the entrance. Open them up and you'll receive Boogle Bombs. These will prove to be useful to get past certain obstacles later, so be sure to grab them.

Map Title:	Jesgran's Deathrun 2.0
Island Code:	1103-0256-3362
Creator:	Jesgran
Creator's YouTube Channel:	https://m.youtube.com/ jespergran

Jesgran invested more than 400 hours in the creation of this highly detailed deathrun scenario. It's just one of several awesome Creative maps he's created and published.

The map is rather intricate and is filled with a lot of obstacles with solutions that are seldom obvious. Just finding the right path to follow could take you a bunch of tries.

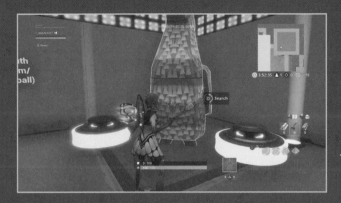

In this scenario, your soldier has fallen into a volcano (oops), and it's your job to help him find his way out. Up to 16 gamers can compete at once, or you can play solo and race against the clock.

One thing is for sure . . . you definitely want to avoid falling into the lava. When this happens, your soldier will be removed from the match and need to respawn.

Map Title:	Jesgran's Deathrun 3.0—Rise from the Ashes
Island Code:	4893-9258-8488
Creator:	Jesgran
Creator's YouTube Channel:	https://m.youtube.com/jespergran

The goal of any challenging deathrun is to get through the map as quickly as possible and move past all of the obstacles intentionally put in your path.

On Jesgran's YouTube channel, you'll find several run-throughs for this map that offer useful clues for how to reach the finish line successfully. Even when you know the best path to take, this deathrun is still challenging to complete.

To achieve success in this deathrun, Jesgran forces gamers to use specific items, like Impulse Grenades, Speedpads, Grapplers, and Ballers in rather innovative ways.

As you approach many checkpoints, the direction to travel next will be somewhat obvious.

Sometimes, figuring out where to leap next will be tricky. One wrong move and your soldier will perish. Sure you'll respawn, but this will set you back a bit and waste valuable time.

Map Title:	Looming Llama
Island Code:	1090-0783-2499
Creator:	st0rmh4wk (StormHawk)
Creator's YouTube Channel:	www.youtube.com/channel/UCo5QJJbcm780xLMxThj-MmQ

This is a "free for all" map where multiple gamers can participate in combat. What's unique about this map is the creative way it uses Prefab buildings that have been extremely well customized and redesigned using many different metal items from the various Galleries in *Fortnite: Creative*.

According to this map's animated trailer (www.youtube.com/watch?v=PljLCH8aRZg) more than 60 hours of hard work went into the creation of this map. The end result is a massive structure that looks like a mechanical spider that is 21 blocks wide, five blocks long, and 10 blocks high. It has a wingspan of 16 blocks. The coolest thing about this massive structure is that it's fully playable.

Chests containing weapons, ammo, and other goodies are strategically placed throughout the map. Some are visible and out in the open, but others you'll need to seek out through exploration.

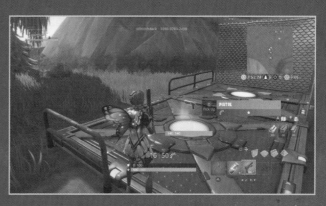

Using its multiple entrances and exits (on either side, through its mouth, and within the tail), soldiers can enter into the mechanical spider, climb on top of it, and make their way below it during battles. When inside the giant metal creature, the layout is well suited for close-combat battles, since there are plenty of objects to crouch behind for cover, places to hide, and locations from which surprise attacks can be launched.

Scattered throughout the map are an assortment of Item and Weapon Spawners that'll help your soldier build up an arsenal.

Your objective is to defeat the other soldiers, so the more people you invite to participate in the match, the more exciting it'll be.

Map Title:	Lordly Labyrinth
Island Code:	1991-9282-9857
Creator:	Jesgran
Creator's YouTube Channel:	https://m.youtube.com/jespergran

In this map, Jesgran has created a detailed and intricate hedge maze with a few buildings within it.

Lordy Labyrinth was designed to fit within Fortnite: Battle Royale's The Block. *Drop into this map and see how far you can get within the five-minute and thirty-second time limit. Yes, there is a finish line . . . but can you find it?*

When you reach one of the castles, climb up as high as you can so you can get the lay of the land and determine which direction within the maze to travel next.

While walking through the maze, you can't climb up on the hedges themselves, but you'll occasionally come across an object, such as a log, that you can stand up on. Stand on the object and then jump up and down to see above the hedges.

Once inside the maze, use the mini-map to help guide you through it. Even with the help of the map, however, you'll still encounter many dead ends and often find yourself traveling around in circles.

Map Title:	Mario Kart Rainbow Road Race
Island Code:	2668-3299-2351
Creator:	FalconStrike1998 (FalconStrikeFilms)
Creator's YouTube Channel:	www.youtube.com/channel/UC9PEsf1QHNZgu029Ow8Q7Mw

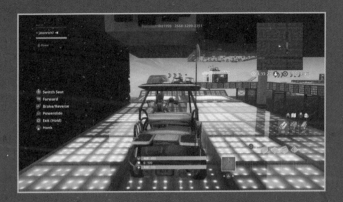

The course itself is filled with obstacles. Here, if you stay in the right lane, you'll travel directly under a Trap and perish. The safe route is the left lane.

The Mario Kart racing game on the Nintendo SNES is a classic. If you accidently drive off the track, you'll need to take an extended detour to find your way back. Meanwhile, if you run into an obstacle, your soldier will be removed from the track and you'll need to respawn.

Check out the animated trailer for this map on YouTube (www.youtube.com/watch?v=olyM41UHcpI).

If you speed over the ramp that's ahead, you'll fall and crash into a ditch. Stay in the right lane here.

In this map, FalconStrike1998 has recreated a popular track from Mario Kart using the tools available from Fortnite: Creative. Play alone or with your online friends to experience more intense ATK racing excitement.

Here's another example where if you're not paying attention, you'll drive right under a Trap and be eliminated from the match. As you approach this straightaway, stay to the extreme left.

Sometimes crashing will result in your soldier needing to respawn. There are usually replacement vehicles nearby that your soldier can hop into, but the clock keeps ticking. Of course, it's possible to flip your ATK as well, which will also cost you valuable time, but won't get you eliminated from the race.

During the match, you're surrounded by water, which has its own set of challenges. As for weapons, there are cannons and your soldier's Harvesting Tool—that's it.

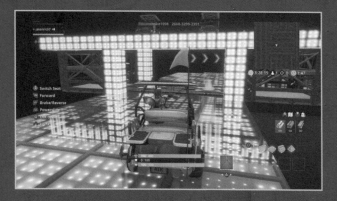

This map is challenging as a one-player race, but it's totally lit when you race against a bunch of online friends.

Get to a level on your platform that gives you a clear line of sight to an opposing platform, and then push your cannon into place to line up your cannonball shots.

Map Title:	Raft Wars
Island Code:	9026-2925-8175
Creator:	azaliak_iphone
Creator's YouTube Channel:	www.youtube.com/watch?v=D1Q9lI6dJJU

Take on the role of a pirate and use only Cannons from *Fortnite: Battle Royale* season 8 to defeat your enemies on nine different platforms, rafts, and boats. The last soldier alive is declared the winner.

There are multiple cannons on each platform. Work with the ones that'll allow you to cause the most damage. If the need arises, have your soldier leap into the water and travel toward a neighboring platform. By staying underwater, however, your soldier's Health meter will get depleted, so move fast.

Map Title:	Sky Royale!
Island Code:	4151-6253-9143
Creator:	Jesgran
Creator's YouTube Channel:	https://m.youtube.com/ jespergran

This scenario is described by its creator as a "the perfect combination between the classic Sky Wars mini game and Battle Royale." When you reach the map, be sure to access the menu and choose a team.

Get ready for some intense fighting as you participle along with between two and 15 other gamers.

This map is comprised of a bunch of tiny islands. To succeed, you'll need to island hop. Use the resources you get from chests to do your building but use your resources sparingly. You'll be able to collect just enough wood, stone, or metal to build bridges or ramps that'll get your soldier from one island to the next with little or no resources left over.

Start each match by locating all of the chests on your tiny island, but hurry up, because the storm is about to form and drive you toward the center of the map.

Each game lasts about four minutes. After about one minute, your soldier gets pushed toward the middle island by the storm. If you don't have the resources to build a bridge and island hop, you'll perish in the storm.

Map Title:	Snipers vs. Quadcrashers
Island Code:	4940-8228-6728
Creator:	RealJosherzz
Creator's YouTube Channel:	www.youtube.com/channel/UCYn7f6D12HjZZvFpe-v9tpA

A giant hill with a platform on the bottom has been created as the setting for this Snipers versus Quadcrashers battle. Check out the animated trailer for this map on YouTube (www.youtube.com/watch?v=bGTB39gvOXw).

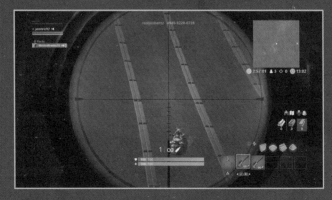

The enemy drivers will be moving, so you'll need to practice shooting at and hitting moving targets. (This is awesome practice for when you're using a Sniper Rifle in Fortnite: Battle Royale.)

If you become a Sniper, at the start of the match, open the nearby chest and arm yourself with some Sniper Rifles.

The drivers will speed down the hill and attempt to knock the Snipers off the platform. At the bottom of the hill, hop into a Quadcrasher and then drive to the top of the hill.

As the Sniper, you'll then stand on the bottom of the hill and must shoot at enemy soldiers who are driving Quadcrashers down the hill toward your soldier.

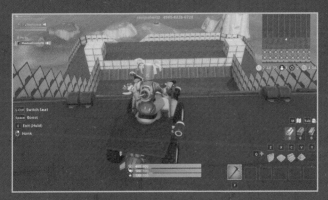

At the top of the hill, a Sniper can see you, but you'll need to line up your vehicle and choose the best starting location to race down the hill.

Map Title:	Snipers vs. Runners
Island Code:	7352-4203-8482
Creator:	Bludrive
Creator's YouTube Channel:	www.youtube.com/ channel/UCJ2_ fYZTg8okhtDzcflBegg

Bludrive is the designer of many maps that he's published using *Fortnite: Creative*. Snipers vs. Runners is just one example of his work. If you're interested in creating your own maps, be sure to check out Bluedrive's YouTube channel, because he offers dozens of tutorial videos, as well as animated trailers for his most popular maps.

As you're racing down the hill, keep an eye on your target and try to steer your Quadcrasher so the vehicle lines up perfectly with a Sniper before going airborne.

At the start of this match, at least one player needs to hit the Menu button and switch teams to become the Sniper.

The bottom of the hill will approach quickly for the Quadcrasher driver. There's a small ramp at the bottom that'll allow the vehicle to go airborne. By this point, you need to have your vehicle lined up to smash into your target—before the Sniper is able to target and shoot your soldier.

The Sniper should approach the chest and grab a weapon, such as the Bolt-Action Sniper Rifle.

The Sniper then needs to position themselves with a clear line of sight to the maze, and then locate their target(s), who are the runners trying to get through the maze.

Even without the Sniper shooting, getting through the maze quickly is rather challenging, since it's easy to get lost. The runner has no weapons or items at their disposal except for their Harvesting Tools, which is not useful on this map.

Map Title:	Super Baller Swing!
Island Code:	7224-1806-6161
Creator:	Swiftor
Creator's YouTube Channel:	www.youtube.com/user/swiftor

The other player is the runner. (This map supports multiple runners.) Their goal is to reach the finish line of the maze in five minutes or less, without being shot by the Sniper.

This map was designed as a race to be experienced while driving a Baller. The track is colorful and loaded with challenges. Check out the animated trailer for this map on YouTube (www.youtube.com/watch?v=1RGVKG5ats4).

The runner is confronted with a rather intricate, multi-level obstacle course that contains plenty of challenges. Bluedrive made good use of Half Damage Rails and Chiller tiles to create roadblocks. One wrong turn or leap, and your soldier will get catapulted off the ledge and need to respawn.

The objective is to roll and swing around and be the first to collect 2,000 points in order to win.

Grabbing certain objects, like Toilet Paper, Spheres, Puzzles, and Coins will earn you extra points.

Map Title:	Swiftor's Musical Chairs!
Island Code:	7121-7065-9582
Creator:	Swiftor
Creator's YouTube Channel:	www.youtube.com/user/swiftor

This is a 16-gamer map that'll make you think you're at a child's birthday party playing Musical Chairs, but in this case there's a *Fortnite* twist.

A few areas of the course are easy to navigate through, so you can pick up speed and make better time. However, if you accidently leave the course (which is easy to do if you don't maintain full control over the Baller), you'll be eliminated from the match and need to respawn back at the start. You'll discover that perfect timing using the Baller's Grappler is as essential as good driving to achieve success.

At the start, the soldier in the middle (the leader) will begin to dance, while up to 15 other gamers run around the row of 14 chairs. When the leader stops dancing, all of the other soldiers must quickly find a seat. The soldier who can't find a seat is eliminated by the leader, and the 14 remaining soldiers will play another round—this time with 13 chairs available. (The leader must remove a chair after each round and after eliminating one of the contestants). Rounds continue until there's only one soldier and one chair remaining.

Many areas of the course get a bit tricky. Perfect timing and the ability to maintain control over your Baller becomes essential if you want to stay on the track.

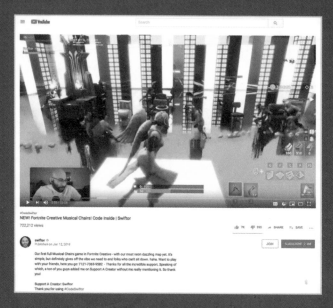

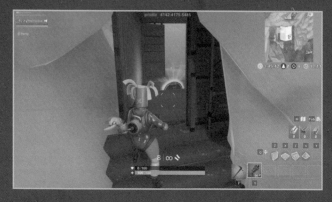

Check out the promo video and demo (featuring 16 players) of Swiftor's Musical Chairs! on YouTube (www.youtube.com/watch?v=2o2vkn3_Vd0).

Map Title:	The Scorpion King
Island Code:	4142-4175-5485
Creator:	Prudiz
Creator's YouTube Channel:	www.youtube.com/user/prudiz

This is a death match scenario with a visually stunning design that allows up to 16 gamers to compete. The last person standing is the winner.

During your exploration, try to collect as many golden Fortnite coins as you can. They're skillfully hidden throughout the island– particularly within the massive scorpion-shaped area where a lot of the fighting action takes place.

Get ready to pummel your opponents as you explore this massive ice structure and smaller structures that surround it. At the start of the match, your soldier will freefall onto the island.

Shockwave Grenades (found within Loot Llamas) can serve you well during this match, so grab one and you'll have an infinite supply.

Scattered throughout the map are chests. You'll definitely want to open these to build up your soldier's arsenal.

Because of its incredible appearance, you'll definitely want to explore this map and make your way up into the ice scorpion. However, first and foremost this map was designed to be a death match, so be ready to confront enemies and fight!

The most exciting thing about this map is the ice structure that you can climb on top of and explore inside. That is, if you can find the way in.

Map Title:	THP Skater Warehouse
Island Code:	1654-0324-7788
Creator:	sirbongsalot69x
Creator's YouTube Channel:	www.youtube.com/ watch?v=x1h-eM0fqbg

This solo map is all about grabbing a hoverboard and skating your way through the skatepark. The "THP" in the title stands for "Tony Hawk Pro."

Collect golden Fortnite coins and perform as many tricks as you can muster before the countdown timer hits zero.

Take advantage of the Hoverboard's Boost to pick up speed and go airborne. Perform tricks successfully to earn points. Crash or wipe out, and you'll be penalized.

Spending time navigating around this map while riding a Hoverboard offers excellent practice for when you need to get around the island and outsmart enemies anytime you're playing Fortnite: Battle Royale.

Map Title:	World Cup Challenge Map
Island Code:	9840-3398-3830
Creator:	Prudiz
Creator's YouTube Channel:	www.youtube.com/user/prudiz

This was one of the solo player versus environment (PvE) scenarios Epic Games used as a qualifier map for the 2019 *Fortnite* World Cup Creative Trials, which lead up to the *Fortnite* World Cup. Put your gaming, shooting, and survival skills to the test as your soldier gets transported to an apocalyptic world.

You're given just four minutes to navigate around, quickly gather an arsenal of weapons, blast away as many of the zombies and sentries as you can, while successfully locating and shooting at defined targets and collecting bacon.

Each time you defeat a zombie, eliminate a sentry, or collect a strip of bacon, you earn points. Your objective is to earn the highest score possible by the end of the four-minute period. Your soldier will respawn (with all of the weapons and items they've already collected) each time they're eliminated from the match, but needing to respawn wastes valuable time.

Once you start this match, your first objective is to find and grab at least one weapon and some ammo. You have mere seconds before computer-controlled enemies will begin approaching your location.

After you've been in this match for just a few seconds, the zombies and sentries will start approaching in groups. Wait too long to defeat or outrun them, and you'll quickly get outnumbered, surrounded, or overrun.

Keep moving! Your main goal is to collect bacon and hit shooting targets (as opposed to defeating zombies and sentries), so begin your search and try to avoid getting surrounded by or backed into a corner by your enemies.

On the plus side, all weapons, items, zombies, sentries, and bacon strips respawn in the same locations, at the same time intervals, each time you experience this match, so each time you try out this scenario, remember where things are and try to memorize the timing patterns of everything. The more you can anticipate, the further you'll get each time you repeat this scenario.

To eliminate groups of zombies at once near the start of this game, grab a weapon and ammo and then climb up the nearby stairs to achieve a height advantage. As the zombies approach, eliminate as many as possible. As they come around the bend and start climbing the stairs to reach you, jump down and head to your next location in search of targets and bacon.

In terms of level of difficulty, the basic zombies are easier to eliminate than the golden monsters (who are larger, move slower, but more powerful). The sentries are the most difficult to defeat, so you're better off figuring out where their respawn pads are located and avoid those areas as much as possible.

Be on the lookout for the different types of shooting targets. Successfully shooting targets and collecting bacon generates more points than eliminating enemies.

Bacon can often be found on higher or lower levels of buildings or structures. Don't just focus on what you see at ground level. Look up to find the glowing bacon and then figure out the best way to reach those locations while encountering the least resistance.

It's a large map, so try to avoid allowing the zombies to surround you. The path in front of you may be momentarily clear, but this is usually when the zombies will quickly approach from behind or they'll flank you from the sides. Stay aware of your surroundings instead of just focusing on what's ahead.

According to Prudiz, the map's creator, at the end of the World Cup Trials when this map was featured, the high score for one match (time limit: four minutes) was 11,215 points. Can you beat it?

This is one of the best *Fortnite: Creative* maps that have been published to date. If you like this one, Prudiz has published more than 20 others, including several that have been featured by Epic Games within The Block (found within *Fortnite: Battle Royale*) and four more that have been featured in Creative mode. In addition to his YouTube channel, you can follow him on Instagram (@prudiz.map.creator).

 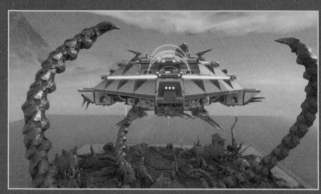

Starship Omega is another of Prudiz popular maps (map code: 2644-1650-6876). It's a visually stunning, highly detailed, "free for all" fighting map for up to 16 players.

The Stacton Village Incident (map code: 6471-2426-71830) is yet another Fortnite: Creative map that can be considered one of Prudiz's masterpieces. It's designed for solo or duo game play, and it's a player versus environment (PvE) adventure map that's loaded with surprises. While the action is intense, the scenery is beautifully designed.

In this map, zombies are everywhere, and they need to be eliminated. Be on the lookout for hidden entranceways and search everywhere. According to Prudiz, you'll definitely need to collect and use Health items to stay in the match and achieve success. The sentries are the most difficult to defeat. They remain hidden until they launch surprise attacks.

As you explore, watch out for Traps, and be prepared to encounter an End Boss. If you keep moving and pay attention to your surroundings, you have a chance to survive. Prudiz plans to create multiple Stacton Village episodes, so keep your eyes peeled for those as well.

Once the match begins, you have just a few seconds before the storm forms and forces your soldier to keep moving forward. Grab the random weapon or item that appears near the starting point and then book it!

Map Title:	Zone Wars to the Future
Island Code:	2080-7366-8235
Creator:	Snownymous
Creator's YouTube Channel:	Snownymous publishes his maps on FortniteCreativeHQ.com

This map is a multi-player obstacle course that's also part deathrun. It offers plenty of combat opportunities if you experience it with online friends.

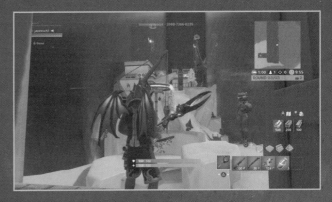

The path you need to follow isn't always obvious, and you'll probably be distracted if you encounter enemies who start shooting. You'll likely need to re-start this map a bunch of times until you get acquainted with its layout and figure out the safest way to avoid the storm and stay safe from enemies.

You have 10 minutes per Round (if you don't get eliminated sooner) to see what this map has to offer.

Aside from walking, running, and jumping, look for ways that'll help your soldier cover a lot of terrain quickly. A geyser will do the trick near the start of the match.

SECTION 4

FORTNITE: CREATIVE RESOURCES

On YouTube (www.youtube.com), Twitch.TV (www.twitch.tv/directory/game/Fortnite), Mixer (www.mixer.com/browse/games/70323/fortnite), or Facebook Watch (www.facebook.com/watch), in the Search field, enter the search phrase *"Fortnite: Battle Royale"* or *"Fortnite: Creative"* to discover many game-related channels, live streams, and prerecorded videos that'll help you become a better player.

Many of the more accomplished gamers who are part of Epic Games' Support A Creator program publish animated trailers for each of their maps, which you can typically find on YouTube, or featured within the independent websites that promote Creative maps.

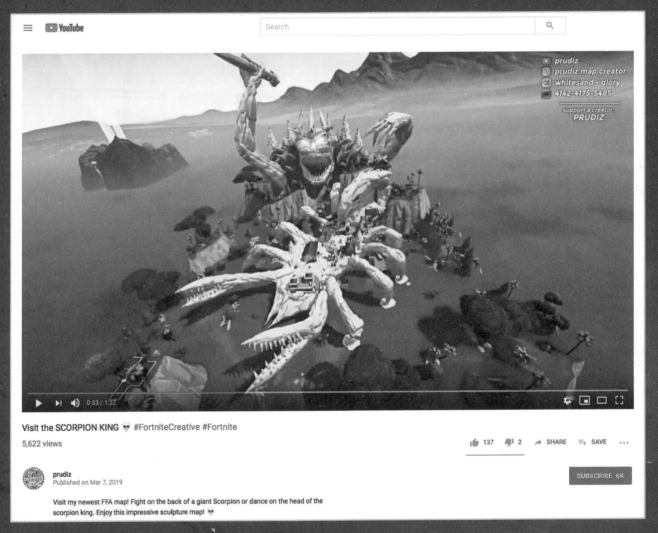

Shown here is the animated trailer for The Scorpion King map created by Prudiz. Watch the full video here: www.youtube.com/watch?v=hx9GOXqbE80.

Also, be sure to check out the following online resources related to *Fortnite: Battle Royale* and *Fortnite: Creative*:

WEBSITE OR YOUTUBE CHANNEL NAME	DESCRIPTION	URL
Best *Fortnite* Settings	Discover the custom game settings used by some of the world's top-rated *Fortnite: Battle Royale* players.	www.bestfortnitesettings.com
Corsair	Consider upgrading your keyboard and mouse to one that's designed specifically for gaming. Corsair is one of several companies that manufactures keyboards, mice, and headsets specifically for gamers.	www.corsair.com
DropNite Popular Maps Directory	An independent database of popular *Fortnite: Creative* maps.	https://dropnite.com/popular-maps.php
Epic Game's Official Social Media Accounts for *Fortnite*	Visit the official Facebook, Twitter, and Instagram Accounts for *Fortnite*. Be sure to use the **#FortniteCreative** hashtag to find specific Twitter discussions and Instagram posts covering this game play mode.	Facebook: www.facebook.com/FortniteGame Twitter: https://twitter.com/fortnitegame Instagram: www.instagram.com/fortnite
Fandom's *Fortnite* Wiki	Discover the latest news and strategies related to *Fortnite*.	http://fortnite.wikia.com/wiki/Fortnite_Wiki
FBR Insider	The *Fortnite: Battle Royale Insider* website offers game-related news, tips, and strategy videos.	www.fortniteinsider.com
Fortnite Creative HQ	An independent online resource that showcases more than 3,000 Creative maps. Check out the Featured and Trending sections of the website to discover the very best maps.	www.fortnitecreativehq.com
Fortnite Gamepedia Wiki	Read up-to-date descriptions of every weapon, loot item, and ammo type available within *Fortnite*. This wiki also maintains a comprehensive database of soldier outfits and related items released by Epic Games.	https://fortnite.gamepedia.com/Fortnite_Wiki
Fortnite Scout	Check your personal player stats and analyze your performance using a bunch of colorful graphs and charts. Also check out the stats of other *Fortnite: Battle Royale* players.	www.fortnitescout.com

WEBSITE OR YOUTUBE CHANNEL NAME	DESCRIPTION	URL
Fortnite Skins	This independent website maintains a detailed database of all *Fortnite: Battle Royale* outfits and accessory items released by Epic Games.	https://fortniteskins.net
Fortnite Tracker Network	A website that showcases many Creative Maps and provides gamers with the codes to access them.	https://fortnitetracker.com/creative
Fortnite: Battle Royale for Android Mobile Devices	Download *Fortnite: Battle Royale* for your compatible Android-based mobile device.	www.epicgames.com/fortnite /en-US/mobile/android/get-started
Fortnite: Battle Royale Mobile (iOS App Store)	Download *Fortnite: Battle Royale* for your Apple iPhone or iPad.	https://itunes.apple.com/us/app /fortnite/id1261357853
Game Informer Magazine's *Fortnite* Coverage	Discover articles, reviews, and news about *Fortnite* published by *Game Informer* magazine.	www.gameinformer.com/fortnite
GameSpot's *Fortnite* Coverage	Check out the news, reviews, and game coverage related to *Fortnite* that's been published by GameSpot.	www.gamespot.com/fortnite
HyperX Gaming	Manufactures a selection of high-quality gaming keyboards, mice, headsets, and other accessories used by amateur and pro gamers alike. These work on PCs, Macs, and most console-based gaming systems.	www.hyperxgaming.com
IGN Entertainment's Awesome *Fortnite: Creative* Map Codes Listing	Check out all IGN's past and current coverage of *Fortnite*, including their list of the most awesome Creative Map codes.	www.ign.com/wikis/fortnite /Fortnite_Creative_Island_Codes _List_and_Awesome_Creations
Islands-Codes. com	An independent online resource that showcases many popular Creative maps. Use this website's Search tool to find the best maps in a specific category, such as team Deathmatch, Hide and Seek, The Block, Puzzle, or Races.	https://island-codes.com/maps

WEBSITE OR YOUTUBE CHANNEL NAME	DESCRIPTION	URL
Jason R. Rich's Websites and Social Media	Learn about additional, unofficial game strategy guides by Jason R. Rich that cover *Fortnite: Battle Royale*, *PUBG*, *Brawl Stars*, and *Apex Legends* (each sold separately).	www.JasonRich.com www.GameTipBooks.com Twitter: @JasonRich7 Instagram: @JasonRich7
LazarBeam's YouTube Channel	With more than 11 million subscribers, LazarBeam offers *Fortnite* tutorials that are not only informative, but very funny and extremely entertaining. You'll definitely want to subscribe to his YouTube channel!	YouTube Channel: http://goo.gl /HXwElg Twitter: https://twitter.com /LazarBeamYT Instagram: www.instagram.com /lazarbeamyt
Map Codes for the 2019 *Fortnite* World Cup Creative Trails	Obtain the map codes for the Creative maps used by contestants during the 2019 *Fortnite* World Cup Creative Trials.	www.epicgames.com/fortnite/en-US /news/world-cup-creative-trials
Microsoft's Xbox One *Fortnite* Website	Learn about and acquire *Fortnite: Battle Royale* if you're an Xbox One gamer.	www.microsoft.com/en-US /store/p/Fortnite-Battle-Royalee /BT5P2X999VH2
Ninja	On YouTube and Twitch.tv, check out the live and recorded game streams from Ninja, one of the most highly skilled *Fortnite: Battle Royale* players in the world. His YouTube channel has more than 22 million subscribers.	YouTube: www.youtube.com/user /NinjasHyper Twitch: https://twitch.tv/Ninja
Official Epic Games YouTube Channel for *Fortnite: Battle Royale*	The official *Fortnite: Battle Royale* YouTube channel.	www.youtube.com/user/epicfortnite
PC Gamer's Magazine Listing of the Best Custom Map Codes	Access a list of map codes for Creative Maps that the editors of *PC Gamer* magazine believe are among the best.	www.pcgamer.com/ fortnite-creative-codes
Pro Game Guides	This independent website maintains a detailed database of Creative maps.	https://progameguides.com/fortnite /fortnite-parkour-maps-codes-list/
Reddit's Best Creative Map Code Discussion	Take part in an online discussion focused specifically on the best Creative map codes and how to find them.	www.reddit.com/r/FortniteCreative /comments/bclya5/best_website _for_creative_codes

WEBSITE OR YOUTUBE CHANNEL NAME	DESCRIPTION	URL
Reddit's *Fortnite: Creative* Forum	Join thousands of *Fortnite: Creative* enthusiasts in an ongoing discussion that includes tips for creating awesome maps. This is an Epic Games-supported forum.	www.reddit.com/r/FortniteCreative
SCUF Gaming	This company makes high-end, extremely precise, customizable wireless controllers for the console-based gaming systems, including the SCUF Impact controller for the PS4. If you're looking to enhance your reaction times when playing *Fortnite*, consider upgrading your wireless controller.	www.scufgaming.com
Turtle Beach Corp.	This is one of many companies that make great quality, wired or wireless (Bluetooth) gaming headsets that work with all gaming platforms.	www.turtlebeach.com

Let Your Imagination Run Wild!

Unlike *Fortnite: Battle Royale,* when you experience *Fortnite: Creative* there are three very distinct ways to challenge yourself and have fun at the same time.

The first is to invest the time to create a clutch island map that features scenery or a layout you wish the folks at Epic Games would add to the island map featured in *Fortnite: Battle Royale.* Use your creativity and the tools available to create something amazing!

Next, tinker with the options available from the My Island menus to develop a unique, fun, and challenging set of rules for matches that'll take place on your island.

Finally, depending on the goal of the island you've created, invite one or more online friends to experience matches on your island and follow your set of rules. Keep in mind, the match rules on your island do not need to be combat oriented, and the goal does not need to be for a soldier to be the last person alive at the end of the match in order to win #1 Victory Royale.

The objective of your map can be a race, to solve puzzles, to outsmart your adversaries in a game of hide and seek (referred to as a Prop Hunt), or to simply offer a whimsical experience for anyone who chooses to explore your island map.

However, if your map is based around a combat scenario, you can create solo matches where gamers compete against computer-controlled monsters, zombies, or sentries. You can make it so a gamer needs to fight another gamer and achieve a specific objective to win. By tweaking the menu settings from the My Island menus, you're also able to create team-oriented gaming scenarios.

Thanks to the hundreds of tools and menu options offered within *Fortnite: Creative*, what's possible is limited mainly by your imagination (and the one hundred thousand memory unit limit imposed on each island map).

Even if you don't have the time and patience to create your own island maps, there are thousands of maps that your online friends and Support A Creator members have published. These are available for you to experience right now. So, even if you think you've mastered *Fortnite: Battle Royale*'s Solo, Duos, and Squads game play modes, for example, there's a whole new set of gaming skills required to beat many of the island maps available when you launch *Fortnite: Creative*. Countless new experiences are being published every single day.

Get ready to have some fun experiencing *Fortnite: Creative*, and don't forget to check out the custom island maps that many of your favorite *Fortnite* streamers from YouTube and Twitch.tv, like LazarBeam (http://goo.gl/HXwElg), have created and published, or that they use to create highly entertaining and often comical video content that you can watch.

There's a lot to see, do, and experience when playing *Fortnite: Creative*, so when you're ready to take a break from the heart-pounding combat action featured in *Fortnite: Battle Royale*, be sure to check out this game play mode where creativity rules!

Also, be sure to check out the other books in this *Fortnite: Battle Royale Master Combat* series. Each book focuses on a different aspect of the game and is chock full of tips and strategies that'll help you win! For more information about these books, visit: **www.GameTipBooks.com.**

Have fun!